Legal Rights
of Children

NASW PRESS

National Association of Social Workers
Washington, DC

James J. Kelly, *PhD, ACSW, LCSW, President*
Elizabeth J. Clark, *PhD, ACSW, MPH, Executive Director*

Legal Rights of Children
General Counsel Law Note

Carolyn I. Polowy, JD
NASW General Counsel

Sherri Morgan, JD, MSW
NASW Associate Counsel

Alison Keller-Micheli
Law Clerk

W. Dwight Bailey
Law Clerk

National Association of Social Workers
Legal Defense Fund

NASW Press

Cheryl Y. Bradley
Publisher

Lisa M. O'Hearn
Managing Editor

Crystal McDonald
Marketing Manager

*This project was funded in part by the
Aileen Neely bequest to the
NASW Legal Defense Fund.*

Table of Contents

Introduction 1

Legal Status of a **Child** 3

  Legal Status Related to Age 3

    Age of Majority 3

    Emancipated Minor 3

    Mature Minor 4

  When Does Age Affect a Child's Rights? 4

    Consent to Treatment and Disclosure of Confidential Information 4

      Areas in Which Minors May Consent to Treatment 4

      Applicable Standards for Consent to Disclosure of Confidential Information and Parental Access 6

      Right to Sue 7

      Minor's Ability to Contract 7

      Right to Educational Services 8

      Competency to be a Witness 8

      Right to be Free from Abuse or Neglect 9

The Child's Legal Status Related to **Families/Relationships** 13

  What is a "Family?" 13

  Reproductive Technology and Surrogacy Laws 14

  Foster Care 16

  Adoption 19

  Divorce and Child Custody 20

    Admissibility of Social Worker's Testimony on Child Custody Issues 20

      Social Worker as Expert Child Custody Witness 20

      Social Worker as a Fact Witness in a Custody Case 23

    Legal Standards for Awarding Custody 24

    "Best Interests of the Child" Standard 24

      The wishes of the child as a factor 25

      Maternal preference 25

      Primary caretaker as a factor 26

Joint Custody in the "Best Interests of the Child" 26
    Consent to treatment—Is joint consent necessary? 26
    Noncustodial parents' access to therapy records. 27
  Child Custody Arising from Same-Sex Relationships 28
Child Visitation. 29
Child Support. 30

The Child and the **Court Systems** 33
  Family Court Process 33
  Guardian *Ad Litem* Process 34
    Role of the Social Worker 34
    Release of Clinical Records to the Guardian *Ad Litem* 35

Conclusion 37

Appendices 39

Appendix A:
  Minors' Ability to Make Medical Decisions 41

Appendix B:
  Minors' Competency to Testify 55

Appendix C:
  Appointment of Guardian *Ad Litem* Laws 61

Appendix D:
  Child Custody Laws 81

Appendix E:
  Noncustodial Parent Access to Records 87

Endnotes 97

Introduction

The National Association of Social Workers (NASW) developed this law note to aid social workers who work with children and families. For social workers providing professional assistance to children, it is helpful to have a general understanding of the legal issues that underpin the determination of a child's rights. Because family law is primarily state law, this law note highlights the various approaches taken by states concerning children's legal rights.

First, this document addresses the legal status of a child, and how age affects a child's rights, including the following: the right to sue, the right to make treatment decisions concerning the child's care, the right to contract, the right to educational services, and the right to be free from abuse and neglect. Next is a discussion of the ways in which a child's legal status relates to the child's family and relationships. The complex legal issues surrounding a determination of what constitutes a "family" or a "child" in the 21st century are also reviewed, as are adoption laws, the foster care system, divorce and child custody, visitation, and support.

This law note also includes a discussion of the admissibility of social workers' testimony on child custody at custody hearings, and also provides social workers with information concerning the family court processes in which they might find themselves interacting with child clients. Finally, five appendices are included at the end of the law note, providing the following:

- state-by-state information about a minor's[1] ability to make decisions regarding healthcare;
- the right of noncustodial parents to access a child's health records;
- a state-by-state summary of child custody laws;
- a state-by-state summary of guardian *ad litem* statutes; and
- a summary of state laws regarding a minor's competency to testify.

The information and resources provided in this document offer an introduction to various legal issues affecting social workers' practice with children and families. **The discussion is not exhortative and should not be used as a substitute for consultation with an attorney in the jurisdiction in which the child or family is located.** Additional information about legal issues of interest to social workers can be found on the Web pages prepared and updated by the NASW Legal Defense Fund at **http://www.socialworkers.orgildf/defaultasp**.

Legal Status of a Child

Legal Status Related to Age

Age of Majority

In the United States an individual is considered a minor until reaching the age of majority, the age at which an individual becomes a legal adult (a state-by-state summary of the age of majority is offered in Appendix A). The age of majority is established by statute in each state. Historically, the age of majority varied among the states, but today, the vast majority of states have established that an individual becomes a legal adult at age 18.[2] Only five states have statutes that specify legal adulthood as an age other than 18. Alabama and Nebraska both establish the age of majority at 19 years of age;[3] and the age of majority remains at 21 in Colorado, Mississippi, and Pennsylvania.[4] In addition, at least five states specify that individuals who marry while under the age of 18 are legal adults.[5] Finally, the age of majority statute in Wisconsin provides that an individual is considered a legal adult for the purposes of a criminal or civil investigation or prosecution at the age of 17.[6]

The idea of children's rights is a modern innovation. Generally children do not have the same rights—or responsibilities—as do adults. The rationale for children's restricted rights is that affording children the same rights as adults would interfere or conflict with parents' constitutional rights to make child-rearing decisions concerning their children.[7]

Historically, children were considered the property of their parents. As such, parents "could decide how to care for them and whether they lived or died."[8] However, beginning in the late 19th century, with the child protectionist movement, many states began to intrude upon parental rights by authorizing social welfare agencies to ensure the "humane treatment, adequate care, and proper education" of children.[9]

Child protectionism, combined with increased knowledge about child development, led many states to extend various rights and protections to children. Each jurisdiction may specify the rights available to minors—such as the right to marry, the right to contract, the right to sue or be sued, or the right to legal representation. In recent years, however, courts and legislatures have been more willing to provide children increased rights and protections in certain circumstances.

Emancipated Minor

Emancipation "removes a minor from parental authority and ends parental obligations."[10] Most commonly, a child becomes emancipated upon reaching the age of majority. Individuals under the age of majority are not generally considered legal adults and are not provided the same rights as adults. However, a child can petition a court to be declared an "emancipated minor." Many states have statutes that provide the procedure through which minors may become emancipated.[11]

To become emancipated, a child usually demonstrates that he or she has the capacity to be self-sufficient and to manage his or her own affairs.[12] Generally, getting married, enlisting in the armed forces, or becoming economically self-supporting is sufficient to effect emancipation through a court order.[13] An emancipated child can make all decisions normally made by an adult.

Mature Minor

The "mature minor" doctrine is "another evolving exception to the presumption of the legal incompetence of children and the general requirement of parental consent to the treatment of minors."[14] A "mature minor" is an unemancipated adolescent who demonstrates sufficient intelligence to understand the risks or consequences of medical treatment, such that the adolescent may consent to the treatment.

Only a few states, including Arkansas and Nevada, have adopted statutes that allow "mature minors" to consent to all forms of medical treatment,[15] or have acknowledged adolescents' common law right to make medical decisions.[16] The U.S. Supreme Court has not yet declared the mature minor doctrine applicable to treatment decisions outside of the reproductive rights context.[17] For a discussion of minors' rights regarding reproductive health and other health issues where parental consent is not required prior to treatment, see the discussion *infra* "Consent to Treatment and Disclosure of Confidential Information".

For clinical social workers treating children, parental consent remains an issue requiring consideration and review. Ideally, the written consent of both parents to the treatment of a minor would be obtained before treatment begins. Variations on the ideal are reviewed and discussed below.

When Does Age Affect a Child's Rights?

Consent to Treatment and Disclosure of Confidential Information

As a general rule, minors are presumed legally incapable of providing or withholding consent to medical procedures or mental health treatment. This rule exists to protect parents' constitutional rights to make child-rearing decisions concerning their children.[18] Exceptions have been carved out in certain areas, though, to facilitate decision making in specific circumstances.

Areas in Which Minors May Consent to Treatment

Legislatures and courts have created exceptions to minors' inability to give informed consent.[19] (A state-by-state summary of areas in which minors may make specific health care decisions is provided in Appendix A.) For example, because emancipated minors are considered to have the same rights and responsibilities as adults, they may make treatment decisions regardless of legal age or parental consent.[20] Furthermore, the Supreme Court extended the fundamental right of privacy to minors, concerning the right to terminate a pregnancy and to obtain contraception.[21] Thus, pregnancy is "one area in which the emergent needs of an adolescent trump concerns about parental rights and adolescent incompetence."[22]

Although states may place some restrictions on adolescents' access to abortions by requiring parental notification, the Supreme Court requires that state statutes provide a judicial bypass of any parental notification requirement.[23] Thus, where a state statute requires parental notification before a minor may have an abortion, that statute must also allow the minor to obtain approval from a judge for the procedure as an alternative to seeking parental consent.[24]

Many states have enacted statutes that allow minors to consent to treatment for sexually transmitted diseases, treatment for drug or alcohol dependence, or treatment for mental health issues, regardless of age. Minors in all states may give consent to treatment for sexually transmitted diseases without parental consent.[25] Likewise, minors in 43 states and the District of Columbia may give consent to treatment for drug or alcohol abuse without parental consent.[26] Also, 23 jurisdictions allow minors in need of mental health services to agree independently to such services without parental knowledge or consent, the age of consent for such services varies.[27]

A few states use the common law "mature minor" doctrine, developed in court decisions in specific states, to allow minors to make their own treatment decisions without parental consent.[28] Thus, under the "mature minor" doctrine, a minor "of sufficient intelligence and maturity to understand and appreciate both the benefits and risks of the proposed medical or surgical treatment," may consent to treatment.[29] Furthermore, at least two states, Arkansas and Nevada, have specifically codified the mature minor rule.[30]

Most states have statutes that specifically allow treatment of minors in emergency situations without parental consent.[31] However, social workers should take care when providing treatment for minors in emergency situations, as some states define "emergency" narrowly. Also, states differ regarding the effort that must be taken to contact a minor's parents prior to emergency care. In Delaware, for example, a treating clinician must make a "reasonable effort" to obtain a parent's consent before a minor's consent to treatment is valid.[32]

Treating clinicians who provide treatment without parental consent—in any of the aforementioned situations—should be aware of whether their jurisdictions permit or require them to inform minors' parents of the treatment before, during, or after it occurs.[33]

Applicable Standards for Consent to Disclosure of Confidential Information and Parental Access

Parents' access to information provided during treatment by a child below the age of consent is a matter of parental right and, as a legal matter, does not need to be limited to dangerous or threatening situations.

As children grow and enter adolescence, they acquire some privacy rights as delineated by state law. The Health Insurance Portability and Accountability Act (HIPAA) medical privacy regulations generally defer to state law as to minors' rights regarding disclosure of confidential information. Typically, this is linked to minors' rights to consent to treatment, as discussed above.[34] HIPAA also provides that, if parents of a minor child of any age voluntarily agree that a health care practitioner may keep their child's information confidential, the practitioner may withhold information from the parents.[35] Social workers should consider whether to develop written confidentiality agreements for parents of minors to sign on a voluntary basis, to clarify the understanding of all parties involved in the clinical treatment.

In addition to state and federal laws, professional standards should be considered when disclosing minors' confidential health and mental health information. Under the *NASW Code of Ethics*, confidential information may be disclosed "with valid consent from a client or a person legally authorized to consent on behalf of a client."[36] In the case of minor clients, the consent necessary is that of their parents. Thus, parents may access information to the same extent as if they were clients, unless the disclosure would cause danger or harm to the child, or if the minor has acquired individual privacy rights, as discussed above. Parents may also authorize the disclosure of their children's confidential information to third parties, such as insurers.

When parents divorce, questions are often raised about the individual parents' rights to access their children's medical records. Appendix E provides a state-by-state comparison of laws regarding the rights of noncustodial parents to access their children's records. In most states, absent a court order limiting access, both custodial and noncustodial parents have the right to access their children's medical records.

Social workers should consider when the duty is triggered to notify parents of their minor child's high-risk or dangerous behavior. For practice purposes, the *NASW Standards for the Practice of Social Work with Adolescents* suggests that confidential information may need to be disclosed if there is a

> suspicion of danger to the youth or to others. In all such situations, the
> social worker shall advise the youth of the exceptions to confidentiality and

privilege, shall be prepared to share with the youth the information that is being reported, and shall appropriately address the feelings evoked.[37]

In addition to social work practice standards and ethical requirements that permit disclosure to prevent harm,[38] courts and legislatures have recognized that health care practitioners may be required to breach clients' confidentiality if there is clear evidence that a client or another identifiable person is in imminent danger.[39] This duty was first articulated on the 1976 California Supreme Court case, *Tarasoff v. Regents of University of California,* which held that a psychotherapist had an affirmative duty to warn a potential victim of intended serious harm by a client.[40]

Thus, if there is a clear and present danger to another identifiable individual, a treating clinician must warn the threatened individual, or must take reasonable steps to ensure the safety of an endangered client. Generally, notifying the police is not sufficient.[41] Many states codify this legal doctrine in statutes, whereas others recognize it in case law.[42] The legal doctrine does not distinguish between minors and adults.

Right to Sue

Minors, generally, may not sue or be sued, because they lack legal capacity. Because minors are neither competent to bring an action on their own behalf, nor to defend an action brought against them, they must be represented by legally authorized persons. A legally authorized person may include a minor's parent, guardian, "next friend,"[43] or a guardian *ad litem.*[44] If a legally authorized person does not represent a child in a civil action, then it is within the power of the court to appoint a representative for that child.

In many jurisdictions, the appointment of a representative, or guardian *ad litem,* for the child is provided by statute.[45] (A state-by-state summary of guardian *ad litem* statutes is provided in Appendix C.) Some jurisdictions require that a court appoint a guardian *ad litem* for an unrepresented minor in an action.[46] In other jurisdictions, the court is not mandated to appoint a guardian *ad litem* when a child is unrepresented, so the appointment of a guardian *ad litem* remains within the court's discretion.[47] In some jurisdictions, statutes allowing the appointment of a guardian *ad litem* may limit the scope of the appointment to specific matters. For example, Maine permits a guardian *ad litem* to be appointed to represent the best interests of a minor child in divorce actions,[48] child abuse or neglect actions,[49] and in certain probate proceedings.[50]

Minor's Ability to Contract

Social workers providing treatment to minors should be aware of limitations on the minor's legal capacity to contract. State law may provide clarification regarding the use of parental health insurance or limiting the liability of parents for payment of treatment when a minor consents to care independently. The limitations on a minor's ability to contract are established to protect the child from immature decision making. Thus, if a minor child enters into a business transaction prior to reaching the age of majority, the contract is generally voidable on the basis of lack of capacity. However, some states have enacted statutes limiting a minor's ability to void contracts made during minority. For example, contracts for emancipated minors are generally not voidable.[51] Many states provide that an individual may agree, after reaching the age of majority, to pay any debt incurred during infancy, but that promise must be in writing.[52] Other states allow an individual to disaffirm a contract entered into during infancy, but the individual must restore any property for which a debt was contracted to the person to whom the debt was due.[53] Furthermore, some states that allow a minor to consent to mental health treatment may prevent the incurring of a debt by the minor's parents for the payment of the services.[54] Social workers should be aware that parents' health insurance might not be available to minors who sought mental health or medical treatment without the consent of their parents.

Right to Educational Services

A minor has a right to educational services, including special education services. Although education is not a right protected by the federal Constitution, where a state has undertaken to provide public education to its citizens, education "is a right which must be made available to all on equal terms."[55] Providing public education is a paramount function of a state; however, this responsibility must yield to the constitutional right of parents to make child-rearing decisions concerning their children's education, such as a parent's decision to have a child educated in a private school.[56] Furthermore, although compulsory school attendance laws exist in each state,[57] all jurisdictions allow parents to home school their children under certain circumstances.[58]

The Individuals with Disabilities Education Act (IDEA) ensures that a child with a disability is provided a free, appropriate education in the least restrictive environment at no cost to the child or his or her parents.[59] Under the IDEA, children with disabilities are entitled to services such as transportation, speech pathology, physical and occupational therapy, social work services, and medical services as necessary to permit them to benefit from their education.[60] The full range of legal issues related to children and education cannot be addressed in this publication, but endnote 59 contains additional resources.

Competency to be a Witness

Social workers serve in a variety of roles related to children who, at times, act as witnesses in legal proceedings. For instance, social workers may act as forensic interviewers in child sexual abuse investigations, clinicians for minor clients who need emotional support to cope with legal proceedings, and as guardians *ad litem*. The legal system requires that all witnesses who testify in court are determined to be competent to testify. Generally, children must know the difference between truth and lies, understand the obligation to testify truthfully, know the consequences of lying, and be capable of observing, remembering, and verbally describing events to be competent to testify.[61] However, the legal standard for establishing the competency of a child to be a witness varies by jurisdiction.

States have taken different statutory approaches in resolving the question of the competency of children to testify (See Appendix B for a state-by-state summary). Historically, state statutes prescribed an age above which a child was presumed to be competent to testify and below which the child was presumed to be incompetent to testify. A few states retain the general prohibition against child testimony, but allow testimony in certain circumstances, as in cases of child sexual abuse.[62] Under federal law and most state laws, the age criterion has been abandoned and all witnesses, including young children, are presumed to be competent, absent evidence to the contrary.[63] Thus, a court will determine children's competency to testify on a case-by-case basis.[64]

Additionally, many states have passed legislation to protect child witnesses in the courtroom, especially if they have been victims of child abuse or sexual offenses. For example, in place of in-person testimony by a child, some courts allow a child's previous out-of-court statements to be admitted into evidence,[65] whereas other courts allow previously videotaped statements made by children to be admitted into evidence.[66] Other measures to protect the welfare of a child witness, allowed by statute, may include the following:

- permitting the child to testify through the use of closed-circuit television;[67]
- relaxing courtroom formalities;
- altering the courtroom environment;
- using additional recesses during the child's testimony;
- using anatomically explicit dolls to aid in child testimony;[68]
- allowing the child to speak to the judge in chambers;[69] and
- permitting a support person, such as a parent or guardian, to accompany a child witness during testimony.[70]

Right to be Free from Abuse or Neglect

According to the Department of Health and Human Services Administration for Children and Families, an estimated 2.9 million referrals alleging child abuse or neglect were made to state and local child protective services in fiscal year 2003.[71] That year, approximately 906,000 children were determined to be victims of child abuse or neglect by child protective services agencies.[72] Furthermore, an estimated 1,500 children died in 2003 as a result of child abuse or neglect.[73] NASW's position is that "children have a right to protection from all forms of child maltreatment," and that "children have a right to be treated with respect as individuals."[74] Thus, "the profession of social work [is committed to]...child protection through comprehensive efforts to ensure the safety and healthy development of children."[75]

All states have mandatory reporting statutes that require social workers, among other professionals, to report suspected child abuse or neglect.[76] Social workers must provide the requisite information regarding suspected child abuse according to the reporting statute, regardless of whether or not the information is privileged social worker–client communication. In connection with mandated reporting of child abuse or neglect, states have limited the doctrine of privileged communication to achieve maximum protection of children, reasoning that protecting children generally supersedes confidentiality of communications between social workers and their clients.[77]

The *NASW Code of Ethics* provides an exception to social worker–client confidentiality for disclosure of private information pertaining to suspected child abuse or neglect. Code §1.01 states the following: "Social workers' responsibility to the larger society or specific legal obligations may on limited occasions supersede the loyalty owed clients...(Examples include when a social worker is required by law to report that a client has abused a child...)."[78] Because child abuse continues to be an epidemic in the United States, "the social worker's duty to report will remain an essential part in an enforcement scheme aimed at saving children from abuse."[79]

In addition to the tension between privileged communication and mandatory reporting requirements, conflicts can occur when balancing families' privacy rights and the need to investigate and identify child abuse and neglect to protect children.[80] Social workers and public welfare agencies have defended, in several cases, legal challenges to their rights to investigate reports of suspected child abuse or neglect without first obtaining search warrants.[81] The Fourth Amendment of the U.S. Constitution establishes that searches of private homes by state or public officials are presumed unreasonable without probable cause and a search warrant. The presumption of unreasonableness may be overcome, however, by showing consent or the existence of exigent circumstances requiring entry.

A number of cases involving child abuse investigations have interpreted the facts of given situations to determine the presence of exigent circumstances requiring immediate entry into a home.[82] The cases challenging social workers' rights to investigate child abuse without a warrant present a number of different factual scenarios that affect the legal analysis. Some of the factors affecting the outcome are as follows:

- whether the social worker entered the premises alone or accompanied by a police officer;

- whether the social worker entered the premises freely, or used varying degrees of implied threats to gain entrance;

- whether the social worker removed articles of the child's clothing, touched the child, or used photography to collect evidence;

- whether there was eventually a substantiated finding of child abuse or neglect;

- whether the investigation proceeded with urgency or after a significant delay.[83]

A North Carolina court decision, *In the Matter of Stumbo*,[84] potentially affects (a) the health and welfare of children in that state, and (b) professional social workers' ability to investigate cases of alleged abuse and neglect quickly and efficiently.[85] NASW's Legal Defense Fund, at the request of the Association's North Carolina Chapter, provided financial support for an *amicus curiae* brief in this case.

In *Stumbo*, a social worker investigated a same-day report of a naked, unsupervised two-year-old child seen in the driveway of a home. After a telephone complaint was made, the child's parents prohibited the county social worker from conducting an interview with the child, as was required by Department of Social Services (DSS) regulations. The social worker neither sought entry into nor entered the home. DSS filed a petition to prohibit the parents' interference with—or obstruction of—the child protective services investigation pursuant to North Carolina law.[86]

The intermediate appellate court, the North Carolina Court of Appeals, ruled in favor of the state agency, and determined that the social worker's action in going to the home to investigate the abuse or neglect report did not constitute a "search," warranting Fourth Amendment protection. Furthermore, the court held that a social worker's private interview with a child for purposes of an investigation of neglect or abuse does not constitute a "seizure," warranting Fourth Amendment protection.[87]

However, in an appeal to the North Carolina Supreme Court[88] the court held that there was insufficient evidence in the record to constitute the alleged neglect that triggered the department of social services' investigation.[89] The North Carolina Supreme Court reversed the Court of Appeals' decision without determining whether the social worker's action of coming to the home to investigate the abuse or neglect report constituted a "search," warranting Fourth Amendment protection.

Clearly established law states that, absent probable cause and a warrant or exigent circumstances, social workers may not enter individuals' homes for the purpose of taking children into protective custody. Circuit courts are divided, however, regarding social workers' power to inspect children without warrants.[90] Several cases have permitted social workers to investigate claims of child abuse or neglect without warrants when circumstances made it appear that children were in danger and when evidentiary support existed for such an assessment.[91]

The Child's Legal Status Related to Families/ Relationships

What is a "Family?"

During the 20th century, the word "family" in the United States traditionally meant the "nuclear family."[92] A nuclear family is typically defined as a "kinship group consisting of a father, a mother, and their children."[93] However, the composition of families and households in the United States is changing.

Because of changes in family structure and gender roles during the past century, children became "more likely to experience living in a one-parent family, a mother-only family, a reconstituted family, or a family with one or two working parents."[94] Married couples maintain the majority of U.S. households, but the number of unmarried-partner households, female-family households, male-family households, and multigenerational family households has increased according to Census 2000.[95] Furthermore, grandparent caregivers care for many children. In fact, 2.4 million co-resident grandparents were caregivers for their grandchildren in 2000.[96]

As stated by the U.S. Supreme Court in *Moore v. City of East Cleveland*,[97] "[o]urs is by no means a tradition limited to respect for the bonds uniting the members of the nuclear family. The tradition of uncles, aunts, cousins, and especially grandparents sharing a household along with parents and children has roots equally… deserving of constitutional recognition."[98] Although the family is not beyond regulation, the Constitution protects the institution of the family and choices individuals make concerning the family.[99] The government intrudes on choices concerning family arrangements only to advance permissible state objectives.[100]

In recent years, though, the government has intruded on individual choices concerning families headed by same-sex couples. Despite recent data showing that individuals living with same-sex partners comprise at least 594,391 households,[101] states are regulating the gay and lesbian individuals' right to marry,[102] form relationships, raise and/or adopt children as a couple,[103,104] maintain custody or visitation rights, and inherit from lifelong partners.[105] Gay and lesbian couples are forming households and raising children; but in most states, families headed by gay or lesbian couples are not recognized in social and legal definitions of family.[106]

The *NASW Code of Ethics* states that "Social workers should obtain education about and seek to understand the nature of social diversity and oppression with respect to...*sexual orientation*."[107] Therefore, social workers "need to understand the complex issues that lesbian, gay, and bisexual people encounter within the dominant culture in order to provide services respectful of each individual" and their families.[108]

The family structure continues to evolve in the 21st century. With greater numbers of single-parent families, reconstituted families, unmarried-partner families, multigenerational families, and gay or lesbian families, the traditional definition of family is expanding. Social norms and expectations—and new legal structures— are being reassessed to address these new realities.[109] Social workers' roles include understanding families and knowing what the government "does to and for children and their families."[110]

Reproductive Technology and Surrogacy Laws

New reproductive technologies, including in vitro fertilization, are widely available in the United States, but are not closely regulated. In fact, few states have adopted legislation regulating in vitro fertilization practices at all. Naturally, new reproductive technologies have created a rapidly changing area of family law, in which the very definition of *family* and what it means to be a parent comes into question. Until recently, in contested custody cases—when placement with one parent over another was an issue—the court's major decision was as follows: "What is in the best interest of the child?"[111] Now, "[t]he threshold issue to be determined may be 'who is the parent of the child.'"[112] The difficulty of this determination is magnified in the emerging area of parentage through surrogacy arrangements.[113]

Determining parentage is complicated by the number of actors who may be involved in the birth of a child conceived through in vitro fertilization. These individuals may include the following:

- The sperm provider;
- the ovum provider;
- the mitochondrial donor;
- the "gestator," or surrogate;
- the man who contracted with one or more of these parties with the intention of becoming the child's father; or
- the woman who contracted with one or more of these parties with the intention of becoming the child's mother.[114]

Are the two adults, who "through their careful and intentional planning brought together all the components necessary for procreation," the child's parents?[115]

Or is the surrogate mother the "real" mother,…who provided the environment and nutrition necessary for the child to grow and develop, not to mention bearing the physical burdens of pregnancy," the child's parent?[116] Or could the parents be the individuals who donated their genetic material? With little legislative guidance, the courts created a convoluted branch of family law. This new legal area is indicative of the widening gap between medical technology and the legal concepts of parents' rights and responsibilities, children's rights, and surrogates' rights.

A surrogacy arrangement is, by definition, a contractual arrangement that seeks to terminate the surrogate's parental rights with the child and confirm the commissioning party's parental relationship with the child. The federal government has not yet enacted legislation in the area of surrogacy contracts, but nearly half of the states now have statutes governing surrogacy. The state approaches vary and range, however, from an outright ban on surrogacy arrangements to a recognition and enforcement of surrogacy contracts.[117] Because surrogacy contracts are often viewed as terminating parental rights, when such termination is not in the best interests of children (as is required under adoption or child custody disputes) and because they often raise concerns about "baby selling," some courts have found it difficult to uphold surrogacy arrangements.

There are basically three possibilities courts and legislatures use to decide the issue of who possesses parental rights to a child born as a result of modern reproductive technologies: (1) the intent-based test, (2) the genetic contribution test, and (3) the definition of the surrogate mother as the legal mother.[118] The intent-based test for determining parental rights in a surrogacy arrangement focuses on "the preconception manifestation of assent of the women involved to use their reproductive functions for a common purpose."[119] Thus, when it is not possible to establish parentage under statutory or constitutional guidelines, some courts have looked to the intent of the parties as expressed in the surrogacy agreement.[120]

On the other hand, the genetic contribution test endorses the view of parental rights that gives priority to those individuals who are biologically related to the child.[121] This test is based on the argument that because "individuals possess property rights in the products and organs of their bodies, and a child is the product of an individual's genetic tissue, the individual should possess quasi-property rights in the baby."[122] The third possibility used by courts and legislators to decide who possesses parental rights to a child is to declare the gestational host, or surrogate, the legal mother of the child.[123]

Another legal issue that arose during the past 50 years, as a result of modern reproductive technology, is the status of children of same-sex unions. Current reproductive technology makes it possible for same-sex couples to have children and, therefore, has altered the objection to the recognition of same-sex unions on the basis of "the theory that such nontraditional unions could not fulfill the traditional role of marital families in the reproduction of children."[124]

Following are some examples of arrangements through which same-sex couples use reproductive technology to have children:

- same gender female partners using intrauterine insemination by donor sperm;

- same gender female partners using in vitro fertilization, using donor eggs and donor sperm, to produce pre-embryos for potential implantation;

- same gender male partners using a gestational surrogate, with donated eggs; and

- a [same-sex] couple…gaining access to donated pre-embryos.[125]

In the changing area of modern reproductive technology, social workers should strive to understand the legal issues that confront same-sex couples and their families, including the following: (1) parentage; (2) a non-biological parent's ability to adopt a child;[126] and (3) child custody, visitation,[127] and support[128] concerns upon the separation of same-sex partners. To better assist clients in clarifying their expectations and the factors influencing their choices, social workers providing services to families using new and nontraditional means of having children need to understand the issues their clients face. To avoid future conflicts, clients also need to understand the obligations and risks they are assuming.

Foster Care

Foster care is defined as "a publicly funded child welfare system of organized services for full-time residential caregiving of children whose parents' condition or behavior prevents them from discharging their parental responsibilities."[129] Foster care is intended to be a temporary solution until parents improve their behavior or the child's living conditions. Thus, NASW supports the principle that "services to reunify the child with his or her family should begin immediately."[130]

The foster care system began in 1853, when the New York Children's Aid Society began placing needy and homeless children from large cities in the homes of rural farmers or tradespersons.[131] The governing principles of free foster care and a preference for placement within a family setting were further developed by the Boston Children's Aid Society, which focused on children's individualized needs, the appropriateness of the foster home placement, and supervision of a foster home once a child was placed.[132] As a result, foster care policy became one of family preservation, and placement decisions were made with an eye toward reunifying children with their families. Today, foster care policy focuses on "permanence for children in substitute care" until the child's parents have improved the child's living conditions or until an alternative plan for permanence, including adoption, is determined to be most appropriate.[133]

Child welfare services are administered by the individual states and are regulated through a number of federal programs.[134] In 1997, Congress passed the Adoption and Safe Families Act (ASFA), which requires states to conduct a permanency hearing within 12 months after a child enters foster care.[135] At the permanency hearing a "permanency plan" is developed, in which the child is either returned to a parent, placed for adoption, referred for legal guardianship, or placed in another planned living arrangement.[136] In an effort to rectify problems of children lingering in the child welfare system, ASFA embodies a preference for the expeditious termination of parental rights.[137] However, some critics argue that by amending the "reasonable efforts" reunification requirement found in the prior Adoption Assistance and Child Welfare Act of 1980,[138] policy makers are simply vacillating between two policy preferences: (1) family preservation and (2) the termination of parental rights in the interest of safety and permanence for the child.[139]

To terminate parental rights, the court must determine whether evidence exists that shows the parent is unfit—for example, that there is evidence of parental misconduct or inability. Additionally, the court must decide whether termination of parental rights is in the child's best interest, considering, among other factors, the child's need for a secure and stable home.[140] Because terminating parental rights is considered a serious state intervention into parental authority, a petitioner must establish by clear and convincing evidence that grounds for termination exist.[141] The grounds for termination may include the following:

- substance abuse;[142]
- stagnation;[143]
- abandonment;[144]
- mental incapacity;[145]
- neglect;[146]
- abuse;[147]
- failure to protect the child from abuse by the other parent;[148]
- incarceration;[149]
- crime committed on the other parent;[150] or
- a newborn blood test revealing a controlled substance.[151]

Parental rights termination proceedings are typically initiated by a state social services agency or a state-authorized private foster care agency.[152] Statutes in some jurisdictions allow termination of parental rights if one parent has petitioned to terminate the rights of the other parent.[153] In addition, states may allow termination upon petition by a guardian *ad litem* for the child, by a third party seeking to adopt the child, by grandparents and other extended family members, or by anyone with a "legitimate interest" in the child's welfare.[154] However, some jurisdictions, in an effort to protect natural parents' rights, have denied foster parents the ability to initiate termination proceedings against natural parents.[155]

A final order of termination permanently and irrevocably extinguishes all of a natural parent's legal rights and obligations to the child. Thus, following a termination order, a natural parent has no right to be consulted on the child's welfare, to visit the child, or be notified of the child's whereabouts or the adoption of the child. However, in some jurisdictions, the termination of parental rights to the child does not terminate the child's right of inheritance from natural parents, even after an adoption order has been entered.[156]

One issue concerning children's rights in termination proceedings is whether or not a child may initiate a parental-rights termination proceeding. Traditionally, minor children have been under legal disabilities resulting from their dependent position on their parents and also because giving children constitutional rights tends to displace the parents' constitutional rights. The Supreme Court has recognized that children's constitutional rights are not the same as those of adults and are sometimes subordinate to those of their parents.[157] As a result, the majority of jurisdictions do not expressly allow minors to petition for termination of their parents' rights.[158] Although most courts retain an exclusive focus on parental rights in determinations of the parent–child relationship, a minority do allow minors to initiate termination proceedings.[159]

Another issue concerning children's rights in permanency hearings and court proceedings terminating parental rights is a child's right to legal counsel. The United States Supreme Court has not required that children be appointed legal counsel in termination proceedings, "although the termination concerns the child as much as it does the parent."[160] However, by recognizing that parents may not adequately represent the best interest of their children in termination proceedings, courts have sometimes appointed counsel for children in such proceedings.[161] Other courts deny legal counsel to children in termination proceedings,[162] whereas still others consider children's need for legal representation on a case-by-case basis.[163]

Of significant consideration for social workers after the termination of parental rights is the matter of who will make decisions about the access to or release of a child's records when the child is in the legal custody of a welfare agency. Most states have statutes that specify that the records and information concerning a child in the possession of a child welfare agency are confidential.[164]

However, there is little guidance on who, within a child welfare agency, may access a child's records or make decisions concerning the release of such records. Some statutes or regulations provide that foster care client records may be released "upon the order of the court,"[165] or "when the agency determines that the person has a legitimate interest in the child and it is in the best interests of the child to release the information."[166] For instance, some states expressly allow disclosure of information to a guardian *ad litem* if the child is subject to a court proceeding.[167] Furthermore, some states include an express prohibition against disclosure of information except for purposes directly connected with the administration of the child welfare agency.[168] Social workers should consult with legal counsel to determine the applicable laws in their states that govern access to—or disclosure of—children's records, when they are in the legal custody of child welfare agencies.

Adoption

According to *The Encyclopedia of Social Work,* adoption "creates new families, expands existing families, and engages adoptive parents in the priceless costs and benefits of parenting."[169] Adoptions generally fall within one of the following four categories:

1. stepparent adoption;
2. independent adoption;
3. agency or relinquishment adoption; or
4. intercountry adoption.[170]

For much of the history of the United States, adoption has been regulated on a local level; therefore, great variety exists among states regarding adoption laws.[171] However, as society's view of the family changes—in order to recognize the rights of children at younger ages and to recognize nontraditional individuals as prospective parents—adoption laws are slowly changing.[172]

According to the 2000 Census, 2,058,915 children are living with adoptive parents. Seventy-eight percent of those adoptive children live with two married adoptive parents, while the remaining 22 percent live with a single parent.[173] Many states explicitly ban "discrimination" based on marital status in adoption placement decisions, and a few states have determined that a preference for married couples in adoption decisions is illegal.[174] Same-sex couples may adopt in a number of states, including California, Massachusetts, New Jersey, New Mexico, New York, Vermont, Washington, Wisconsin, and the District of Columbia.[175] The *NASW Code of Ethics* states that "[s]ocial workers should obtain education about and seek to understand the nature of social diversity and oppression with respect to…*marital status.*"[176] The Code is interpreted as supporting individuals' rights to adopt, regardless of marital status and sexual orientation.

NASW policies also support legislation that would "legitimiz[e] second-parent adoptions in same-sex households."[177] However, there has been significant legislation and case law in recent years expressly restricting the rights of same-sex couples to marry and adopt children.[178] At least three states explicitly deny adoption to same-sex couples on the basis of the adoptive parents' sexual orientation.[179] Currently, efforts are underway in at least 16 states to create laws prohibiting the adoption or foster care of children by same-sex couples or gay and lesbian individuals.[180]

Because a large number of same-sex couples are having and raising children, states are increasingly recognizing same-sex couples as parents and/or allowing second-parent adoption by same-sex parents.[181] Advocates of second-parent adoption for same-sex couples argue that it (a) provides increased security for children through entitlement to government benefits if the adoptive parent becomes disabled or dies, (b) guarantees support payments if the child's parents were to separate, and (c) gives automatic custody of a child to the non-biological parent.[182]

A number of states, including California, Delaware, the District of Columbia, Illinois, Indiana, Massachusetts, New Jersey, New York, Pennsylvania, and Vermont, allow second-parent adoptions, without the biological parent losing any rights, if the adoption is in the best interests of the child.[183] In many more states, trial courts have permitted second-parent adoptions.[184] Courts in at least four states, however, have specifically denied second-parent adoptions for same-sex couples.[185]

NASW policy statements oppose legislation that restricts adoption by gay, lesbian, bisexual, or transgender people.[186] In an amicus brief filed in *Sharon S. v. Superior Court,*[187] NASW stated that "[l]esbian and gay people have been inappropriately denied legal rights in numerous ways including the ability to maintain legal ties to their children, and that denial of legal rights legitimizes homophobic acting-out behavior."[188] Additionally, NASW supported the respondent who was seeking to adopt her former domestic partner's biological child. The Association argued that state adoption statutes should be liberally construed to protect children's welfare, and that second-parent adoption benefits children by keeping families intact and promoting stable relationships.[189]

Divorce and Child Custody

Admissibility of Social Worker's Testimony on Child Custody Issues

Social workers may be called to testify in custody proceedings, either as expert witnesses or as fact witnesses. Confusion and anxiety may be generated for the treating clinician if a party to a custody dispute attempts to utilize treatment information as if it were the evaluation or report of an expert retained for the purpose of evaluating and recommending custody. Clarifying the role of the social worker when records or testimony are sought for use in custody proceedings is a necessary step in determining how to respond to legal requests for disclosure of client information.

Social Worker as Expert Child Custody Witness

Expert witnesses are individuals who have developed, through "knowledge, skill, experience, training, or education," an ability to interpret or explain complex information in a given field of practice or study."[190] A social worker serving as a custody expert could be asked by a party to the litigation or by judicial appointment to provide testimony, on the basis of personal observations, about recommended living and visitation arrangements for the child. The social worker also may be asked to draw a conclusion, offer an opinion on the basis of a hypothetical example, or interpret data and facts already in evidence. Some social workers specialize in conducting custody evaluations and generating court reports, and routinely testify about these matters.

If properly qualified as an expert, a social worker's testimony is generally admissible on the issue of child custody in proceedings for adoption, termination of parental rights, and all other child custody proceedings.[191] Courts in some states have directly held or recognized that a social worker's expert testimony is admissible on the issue of child custody.[192] In a few states, however, courts have held that, although the testimony of a social worker in child custody proceedings is admissible, it is not mandatory.[193] Thus, in those states, it would not be an abuse of the court's discretion to disallow social workers to express their opinions on custody. Although it is not mandatory in custody proceedings, the court or one of the parties may request a social worker to act as a "custody evaluator," to determine which party should retain custody of a child. The role of the evaluator in a child custody dispute is different from that of a treating clinician. Because the NASW Code of Ethics states that a social worker's "primary responsibility is to promote the well-being of clients," trying to be both a treating clinician and a custody evaluator raises ethical concerns.[195] It is not unusual for a treating clinician to have more contact with the custodial parent, and thus to create a potential for bias toward that parent—or at least to generate an appearance of bias. If the social worker initially treated the parents together as a family or couple, testifying in legal proceedings for one party or the other would create an impermissible conflict of interest. A social worker retained as a custody evaluator is positioned in a more objective role, without a prior connection to any of the parties to the case.

The custody evaluator usually must meet minimum qualifications to testify as an expert at trial. However, many state statutes are silent regarding individuals permitted to conduct custody evaluations and the qualifications those individuals must have. Generally, the admission of the custody evaluator's testimony as a qualified expert is purely at the discretion of the court.[196] At least one state has established guidelines governing custody evaluations by listing the mental health professionals allowed to conduct the evaluations, without offering guidance on the specialized competence of the individual conducting the evaluation.[197]

In contrast, California's custody evaluator statute states that clinical social workers are qualified to be child custody evaluators,[198] and the 2005 California Rules of Court §5225 enumerates custody evaluators' required education, training, and experience in child and family development.[199] For example, a custody evaluator is required to complete forty hours of initial education and training in various topics, including, but not limited to,

- understanding children's psychological and developmental needs;
- knowing about safety issues that may arise during the evaluation process;
- interviewing or assessing adults, infants, and children;
- applying comparable interview, assessment, and testing procedures that meet accepted clinical, forensic, scientific, diagnostic, or medical standards to all parties;
- learning when to consult with or involve additional experts;
- understanding how to inform each adult party of the purpose, nature, and method of the evaluation; and
- assessing parenting capacity and construct effective parenting plans.[200]

Whether an individual is qualified to conduct a custody evaluation and testify at trial is a matter of significant concern to social work. The *NASW Code of Ethics* states that "[s]ocial workers should provide services...only within the boundaries of their education, training, license, certification, consultation received, supervised experience, or other relevant professional experience."[201] Therefore, to provide adequate services to the child and the court, social workers should ensure that they possess the particular competencies and knowledge required for child custody evaluations.

Social workers who do not have specialized training should not serve as custody evaluators. Published guidelines for various mental health professionals are available for guidance. For example, NASW's Oregon Chapter developed *Model Standards of Practice for Child Custody Evaluation,* approved by the Oregon State Licensure Board of Clinical Social Workers.[202] Also, the American Psychological Association's *Guidelines for Child Custody Evaluations in Divorce Proceedings* states that the individual preparing for the child custody evaluation (1) "gains specialized competence in performing psychological assessments of children, adults, and families and (2) has "[e]ducation, training, and experience and/or supervision in the areas of child and family development, child and family psychopathology, and the impact of divorce on children."[203] Furthermore, the American Academy of Child and Adolescent Psychiatry's *Summary of the Practice Parameters for Child Custody Evaluation* provides a custody evaluator with direction in conducting the evaluation.[204]

Social workers have been qualified as expert witnesses in courts of law, in numerous cases, to testify on various matters related to families.[205] For example, in *In re Adoption/Guardianship No. CCJ14746*,[206] Maryland's highest court held that a certified social worker is qualified to testify as an expert witness in a parental rights case. NASW and other professional social work organizations participated in the case as *amici curiae*.[207]

In this case, a minor child had been placed in foster care after a determination of neglect and upon her mother's conviction and sentencing for theft and possession of a controlled substance. A clinical social worker was called to testify as an expert witness for the Department of Social Services regarding the emotional and mental disorders of both the child and the mother.[208] The circuit court granted the DSS petition for guardianship of the minor child and terminated parental rights. On appeal, the mother contested the recognition of the clinical social worker as an expert witness. The Maryland Court of Appeals affirmed the lower court's ruling, holding that nothing in the social work licensing law bars social workers from providing expert testimony and that social work expert testimony should be evaluated under the same rules applicable to other experts.[209]

Social Worker as a Fact Witness in a Custody Case

As an alternative to serving as an expert witness, a social worker may be subpoenaed[210] to testify as a fact witness in a custody proceeding, because the social worker is the child's treating clinician. Many social workers receive subpoenas to testify in custody proceedings even though they never agreed to act as custody evaluators, and did not foresee the possibility. As fact witnesses, social workers are not automatically exempt from the duty to provide evidence; however, the court may quash (i.e., vacate or annul) the subpoena at the request of one of the parties.[211] Social workers may still be required to testify about factual evidence, but may not be required to testify about their opinions about the facts, as would expert witnesses.[212]

When complying with a subpoena, a social worker who is the treating clinician to one of the parties may be concerned about whether or not the subpoena will require the disclosure of privileged communication or information communicated between the social worker and the client." In *Jaffee v. Redmond*,[214] the U.S. Supreme Court recognized a psychotherapist–patient privilege that encompasses social workers.[215] The Court held that the confidential communications between a licensed psychotherapist and patient during the course of diagnosis or treatment are privileged under the Federal Rules of Evidence in federal court proceedings. The Court further held that this privilege extends to the confidential communications between a licensed social worker and client in the course of psychotherapy.[216]

Although state courts vary, *NASW's Code of Ethics* requires social workers to "protect the confidentiality of clients during legal proceedings to the extent permitted by law."[217] Thus, a social worker must protect the confidentiality of all information obtained in the course of professional service, unless (a) the client has given valid consent to disclosure,[218] (b) the disclosure is required to "prevent serious imminent harm to the client or another identifiable person,"[219] or (c) when laws and regulations require disclosure without a client's consent.[220] To protect clients' confidentiality, social workers may need to file a motion to quash or modify the subpoena, asserting the privilege on behalf of their clients, if consent is not provided. However, a client can, at any time, waive the privilege; in this case, the social worker would be required to release the information.[221]

Determining which parent may waive a child's privilege in contested custody proceedings is particularly complex when the minor is an adolescent, and opposes the disclosure to a parent with whom the minor has a strained or distant relationship. Social workers who have legitimate professional concerns that disclosure of children's records in contested custody proceedings would be harmful to the children should seek legal counsel regarding how to respond to a subpoena requesting such information. This is discussed further in the section below regarding access to records by noncustodial parents in joint custody situations.

Courts vary as to the weight they give to social workers' testimony in custody disputes, particularly if the social workers have not been called as expert witnesses. While not holding that social workers' testimony is inadmissible, one state court has stated that the "hopes and fears of social workers should not be considered by the court" in custody proceedings.[222] This may reflect the differences in the opinion testimony that expert witnesses are permitted to provide, in contrast to the testimony allowed of fact witnesses. Legal counsel for each party will present objections to questions outside of the realm permitted to the social worker witness. Social workers who testify in court cannot generally respond to questions until the presiding judge rules on objections, and any issues of privilege and/or waiver are resolved.

Legal Standards for Awarding Custody

"Best Interests of the Child" Standard

In modern custody law, the "best interests of the child" is the predominant standard. Under this standard, a court considers all surrounding circumstances of each particular case when making custody determinations. Courts and legislatures have enumerated many factors to be weighed in a custody determination, but will not normally give controlling effect to any one. These factors may include: (1) the child's wishes; (2) the parents' wishes; (3) the interaction and interrelationship of the child with his parents, siblings, and other persons who may significantly affect the child's best interests; (4) the child's adjustment to his or her home, school, and community; (5) the mental and physical health of all individuals involved; (6) the parents' characters and resources; (7) evidence of domestic violence; and (8) consideration of who was the child's primary caretaker.[223]

The "best interests of the child" is a gender-neutral standard, intended to result in equitable custody determinations. Because of the historical existence of gender preference in custody determinations, an individual conducting a child custody evaluation should take care to not make determinations based on stereotypes. Social workers engaging in child custody evaluations should be aware of how biases regarding age, gender, race, ethnicity, national origin, religion, sexual orientation, disability, language, culture, and socioeconomic status may interfere with objective evaluations and recommendations.[224]

The wishes of the child as a factor. The child's preference is one of the factors normally considered when making a custody determination. Many courts recognize that, when a child "is sufficiently mature to formulate and express a rational opinion and desire as to his or her custody," the child's wishes should be a factor in the custody determination.[225] However, all factors, including the child's wishes, are subordinate to the child's overall welfare. Therefore, the child's preference as to custody is not a controlling factor, but should be viewed in light of all the surrounding circumstances.

In some jurisdictions, this matter is controlled by statute. Several jurisdictions have adopted statutes that providing that where all other factors are equal (i.e., both parents are equally suited for custody), the custodial preference of a child of sufficient age or maturity is but one factor to be considered.[226] These courts have held that, where both parents are equally fit, the child's custodial preference is entitled to greater weight.

Generally, although jurisdictions differ on the amount of weight that should be given to the child's preference, the initial determination is whether the child is of sufficient age, maturity, and intelligence to make an informed decision on custody. A determination of each child's capacity is conducted on an individual basis. Additionally, many cases suggest that the child's preference concerning custody must be based on good reasons, not on "the desire to escape discipline or restraint,"[227] or on expressed preference that "reflects the influence of others."[228]

Finally, a number of courts have held that, when a custody dispute is between a natural parent and a more distant relative or individual unrelated by blood, the child's wish to be placed in the custody of the non-natural parent will be disregarded.[229] For example, in *Gradwell v. Strausser*,[230] the Pennsylvania Superior Court held that the 15-year-old child's preference to live with her maternal grandparents could not outweigh a parent's *prima facie* right to custody, because persons other than natural parents are "third parties" in child custody disputes and, therefore, lack standing to seek custody.[231]

Maternal preference. Throughout the years, jurisdictions have adopted varying views on how to make child custody determinations, and have adopted approaches "reflecting society's changing perspective of the family relationship."[232] Beginning in the late 19th century, the historical preference for paternal custody was replaced by a presumption in favor of maternal custody, especially for younger children. In recent years, the maternal preference eroded, and many jurisdictions replaced it with the gender-neutral "best interests of the child" standard. However, in the absence of an express statutory provision denoting the equal rights of parents to child custody, jurisdictions differ on their treatment of the maternal preference rule.[233]

Primary caretaker as a factor. A relatively recent development in child custody law is the recognition given by the courts to the parent who is acting as the primary caretaker of the child when making custody determinations.[234] The trend has been to consider the primary caretaker role as one factor among many, and not as the controlling factor in a custody determination. However, the vast majority of courts have given considerable weight to which parent is the primary caretaker of the child when all other factors are equal.[235]

Joint Custody in the "Best Interests of the Child"

Joint custody is an arrangement in which both parents retain custody of the child and jointly make major decisions concerning the child's welfare. Some courts and legislatures have found joint custody to be in the best interest of the child, and have allowed a determination of joint custody.[236] While joint custody awards are expressly provided by statute in most states, some state courts find authority to make joint custody determinations through statutes giving broad judicial discretion in custody determinations.[237]

Joint custody generally includes both joint *physical* custody and joint *legal* custody.[238] Of concern to social workers is how the various states define joint custody, especially when the statutes are unclear.[239] Although most states define joint custody as including physical and legal custody,[240] a few states define joint custody as joint *legal* custody alone,[241] and others expressly allow judicial discretion in awarding joint legal custody, joint physical custody, or both.[242] Additionally, in some states, there exists a preference for an award of joint custody where both parents agree to the propriety of such an award.[243] Only a few states have developed a presumption of joint custody.[244]

Because of the wide variation of custody arrangements that courts may impose, the question of whether both parents retain the ability to initiate or terminate mental health treatment for their minor children in joint custody determinations following divorce is of concern to social workers. Joint legal custody allows both parents to be legally responsible for their children. Unless provided otherwise in the custody decree, therefore, both parents would retain the right to make decisions about the child, even if joint physical custody is not awarded.[245]

Consent to treatment—Is joint consent necessary? An additional issue for social workers to consider in joint custody situations is whether or not consent must be obtained from both parents prior to treating a child of divorced parents. The *NASW Code of Ethics* §1.03(a) and (c) together state that social workers should provide services based on "valid informed consent," and when clients lack the capacity to provide informed consent, social workers should seek permission from "an appropriate third party."[246] In the recent case, *Andrews v. Board of Social Worker Licensure,*[247] the Superior Court of Maine determined that a social worker who had obtained informed consent from only one parent before treating a child of divorce, had not violated the Maine social work licensing laws, which incorporate Sections 1.03(a) and (c) of the *NASW Code of Ethics.*

This case, however, is not controlling in another state. Social workers should exercise caution by assessing the need for both parents to consent to treatment. Additionally, social workers may request copies of divorce decrees or custody orders. In the absence of clarity, social workers may request that the consenting parents sign a statement confirming that they have the legal right to consent to their children's treatment without the consent of any other individuals.

Noncustodial parents' access to therapy records. Another concern for social workers is whether or not a noncustodial parent may access a social worker's therapy records concerning a child client. Most states have enacted statutes that provide noncustodial parents access to at least some of their children's records, unless the court provides otherwise.[248] However, the states vary regarding exactly which records noncustodial parents may access.

Many states have broadly-worded statutes that allow access by the noncustodial parent to virtually all records pertaining to the child.[249] For example, Alabama Code §30-3-154 states: "[A]ll records and information pertaining to the child, including, *but not limited to,* medical, physiological, dental, scholastic, athletic, extracurricular, and law enforcement, shall he equally available to both parents, in all types of custody arrangements."[250] However, some states' statutes are narrowly worded, limiting noncustodial parents to only the types of records listed in the statutes.[251] For example, Nebraska Revised Statutes §42-364(4) states: "[E]ach parent shall continue to have full and equal access to the *education* and *medical* records of his or her child."[252]

Several states do not include noncustodial parent access to child records in their custody statutes.[253] As a result, in these states, the law is silent regarding the records to which noncustodial parents are guaranteed access. Social workers should consult with their attorneys prior to disclosing children's records to noncustodial parents, to ensure that: (a) no court decree restricting parental access to records has been issued;[254] and (b) that the state statutes and/or case law do not require social workers to disclose their records to noncustodial parents. This is especially important in situations of child or spousal abuse prior to divorce, when disclosure of therapy records may place the safety of a child or custodial parent at risk.

In several jurisdictions, children may assert their therapist-client privilege over parents' waivers of a child's privilege.[255] In a 2005 case, *In the Matter of Berg*,[256] the Supreme Court of New Hampshire determined that it is within the trial court's discretion to determine if it is in the best interests of children to have confidential and privileged therapy records revealed to parents.[257] Furthermore, the court held that children have the right to assert their therapist-client privilege with regard to therapy records and parents and, as such, "parents do not have the exclusive right to assert or waive the privilege on their child's behalf."[258] The court reasoned that, "There is a serious risk that permitting parents unconditional access to the therapy records of their children would have a chilling effect on the therapist-client relationship, thus denying the children access to productive and effective therapeutic treatment."[259]

The court's holding that therapists may deny custodial parental access to minor's records if providing the record could "interfere with treatment," could shift an enormous amount of authority in New Hampshire to mental health professionals in derogation of parental rights, if other court decisions concur with *Berg*.[260] This ruling has limited impact beyond New Hampshire, but suggests that, if parents are involved in a custody case, therapists should consider not only whether there is parental consent, but also may consider the effect of the disclosure on the child before deciding whether to take legal steps to block requests for disclosure. The court's holding in *Berg* does not squarely address a parent's general right to access records outside of legal proceedings. Thus, left unanswered among other questions is the issue of whether, in New Hampshire, the same parent could obtain copies of a record for other purposes deemed legitimate by the courts, such as to review the appropriateness of treatment and/or to facilitate a review of the treatment.

Clinical social workers should consider how to address confidentiality when the children of divorced or separated parents enter treatment, even if they are not currently involved in legal proceedings. One option may be for the therapist to notify the parents that the records may not be accessible for litigation purposes if a court determines that disclosure would be detrimental to the child. Another option, available under HIPAA, is for parents to voluntarily sign an agreement to honor the confidentiality of communications between the therapist and child.[261]

Child Custody Arising from Same-Sex Relationships

State law has been slow to recognize the fact that gay and lesbian couples are having and raising children.[262] Because of the lack of statutory guidance concerning children arising from same-sex relationships, an individual who is not the child's biological or adoptive parent may have difficulty finding a legal basis from which to assert custody rights to his or her children.

Some courts have applied various equity doctrines in order to award custody to the same-sex partner of a biological or adoptive parent.[263] Courts have applied equitable parent, *de facto* parent, or psychological parent doctrines to award some form of custody to a same-sex partner.[264] In addition, some courts have awarded custody to a biological or adoptive parent's same-sex partner on the basis that such custody is in the best interests of the child.[265] However, the majority of states place a non-biological or non-adoptive parent in the same position as a mere third party, thus denying a legal basis to seek custody.[266]

In fact, courts have awarded custody to a third party in a dispute between the third party and the former, same-sex partner of the child's legal mother or father.[267] This legal environment creates an added vulnerability for children of same-sex partners that social workers working with such families should be attuned to, both as a clinical issue affecting family dynamics, and as an opportunity to advocate for family preservation when needed.

Child Visitation

Where the custody of a child has been awarded to one parent, a visitation order may delineate the noncustodial parent's visitation rights, such as the parent's right to visit and see the child at the custodial parent's home, or the right to take the child from the home for extended periods of time. The primary considerations in determining visitation rights, in most states, are the welfare and best interests of the child. Some states have developed visitation guidelines to inform judicial discretion in making visitation determinations.[268] However, most states grant noncustodial parents the right to unrestricted visitation with their children unless their conduct poses a risk to the child's safety. Complete denial of visitation is rare.

Furthermore, jurisdictions differ on whether visitation should he denied or restricted even when there is a finding of sexual abuse.[269] A few states have enacted statutes specifically addressing parental visitation in cases of sexual abuse.[270] Although courts differ about whether to restrict or deny visitation, several factors have been discussed by the courts in making visitation determinations, including the following:

- The lack of a credible explanation by the accused parent how the abuse may otherwise have occurred;
- Expert testimony to establish that sexual abuse had occurred;
- The fact that the parent had been subject to a criminal indictment in the past;
- The testimony of the child's physician establishing that the sexual abuse had occurred to a reasonable medical certainty;
- Testimony that the visiting parent may still attempt to abuse the child even during supervised visits;
- The closeness of the relationship between parent and child;

- The child's belief that he or she had been sexually abused regardless of whether abuse had occurred; and
- The completion of counseling by the parent seeking visitation.[271]

All jurisdictions, except the District of Columbia, have enacted statutes that recognize a grandparent's right to visitation with his or her grandchildren.[272] Some states extend the right to bring a visitation petition to other interested third parties when continued contact with the child would be in the child's best interest.[273] However, in recent years a number of courts have held that the grandparent visitation statutes are an unconstitutional infringement on a parent's right to rear and to "make decisions concerning the care, custody, and control of their children."[274] Courts in Alabama, Arkansas, California, Connecticut, Florida, Georgia, Iowa, Maryland, Michigan, New Jersey, South Carolina, South Dakota, Washington, and Wisconsin have made such constitutional determinations.[275]

Legislative changes have been made to the grandparent visitation statutes, to give sufficient deference to parental decision-making concerning visitation to pass constitutional muster.[276] In addition, several state courts have interpreted their state's statutory requirements to avoid a finding of unconstitutionality by mandating a showing of parental unfitness or harm to the child, or by mandating a demonstration that denial of visitation would cause harm to the child.[277] However, several courts have upheld grandparent visitation statutes by finding that the statutes provide sufficient deference to a fit parent's decision-making concerning grandparent visitation with the child.[278] Although states are handling the constitutionality of their grandparent visitation statutes in varying ways, the award of grandparent visitation continues to be an ongoing and important concern for courts, parents, and children.

Child Support

A child has a right to financial support by a biological parent, and child support obligations are enforceable on behalf of a child. A parental support obligation is owed directly to the child, and is independent of the parental relationship and any agreement between the parents.[279] Courts determine support obligations under their statutes based on the child's need for support and the parent's financial ability to contribute to that support.

In all states, child support presumptively terminates at the age of majority.[280] However, in some states, the support obligation ends at either graduation from high school or age 19, whichever is earlier.[281] In other states, child support ends at age 18, unless the child is still attending high school.[282] Some states still require support until the child reaches age 21.[283] Furthermore, even though a court may not require married parents to support their children during college, a court may constitutionally require a divorced parent to provide college support if the support statute so provides.[284] Emancipation, however, typically terminates a parent's support obligations.

Child support statutes vary among the states, and few of them even provide for awards of custody or visitation to a non-biological, non-legal parent, such as a stepparent or a biological parent's same-sex partner. Therefore, biological parents have encountered difficulties in getting courts to award child support from non-biological, non-legal parents. For example, stepparents historically had no legal obligation to provide support to their stepchildren. Today, though, some states impose a statutory support obligation on stepparents—at least while the stepparent is married to the child's biological parent.[285] Furthermore, some states impose a support responsibility on grandparents for children born to the grandparents' minor children.[286]

As the number of same-sex couples raising children continues to grow and gain societal recognition, courts are called upon to resolve legal issues arising from these relationships and their dissolution. One such issue is whether courts should impose child support obligations on a former same-sex partner, if the child was conceived during, or raised by, the partnership. Because courts are progressing toward recognition of non-biological parents and nontraditional families, the next step is to extend those parental rights into parental obligations, particularly child support.[287] Court decisions that impose a support obligation on a biological parent's former same-sex partner enforce a public policy that children need to be protected, regardless of the sexual orientation or marital status of their parents. Since this issue is new to the legal system, the custodial parent has generally relied on various existing theories in family law to support a claim for child support. Those theories have included: (1) *in loco parentis*[288] (2) equitable estoppe,[289] (3) *de facto* parenthood,[290] and (4) breach of contract.[291]

In some states, statutes that were previously inapplicable are now being applied to children of same-sex couples with favorable results.[292] For example, in *Chambers v. Chambers*,[293] the Delaware Family Court determined that, since the child support statute did not define "parent," the court was required to define the term. The court concluded that it could not ignore the events that occurred prior to the litigation, that the former same-sex partner helped fund the biological mother's in vitro fertilization, cared for the child in the same home as the biological mother after the child's birth, and sought visitation rights with the child through the court.[294] Thus, the court concluded that the former partner was the child's parent within the meaning of the Delaware statute.[295] However, two other courts have held that a support statute did not obligate a former same-sex partner of the biological parent of a child to provide support for the child.[296]

The Child and the Court Systems

Family Court Process

Cases involving families and children may be handled by a jurisdiction's general court system or by a unified family court, created in the jurisdiction to hear cases involving families and children. Generally, state court systems are divided into a hierarchy of courts, with each court being responsible for hearing specific types of cases. Thus, different family matters may be divided among various courts. The result is often "a fragmented system that can prove harmful to families."[297]

However, some states created family courts by statute in order to

- offer more consistent and efficient services to families;
- combat overcrowded dockets in the district and circuit courts;
- ensure that court time is used more effectively;
- coordinate all the case management and agency efforts for a single family; and
- benefit children by settling cases in a shorter amount of time.[298]

Social workers managing professional services in cases involving children or families should be aware of their jurisdictions' family court processes. Family courts generally have jurisdiction to hear cases involving domestic or family relationships such as: child neglect; child abuse; juvenile neglect; dependency; paternity of children; adoptions; custody and visitation of children; terminations of parental rights; divorce and related financial issues like child support, alimony, or distribution of property; and domestic violence.[299] Some family courts may also have jurisdiction over juvenile offenses.[300] For example, the Delaware Family Court has jurisdiction over all juvenile offenses except murder, rape, and kidnapping.[301]

Furthermore, family courts often offer children and families alternate dispute resolution programs, such as mediation, divorce education, and drug counseling programs.[302] The rationale for providing such services is that emphasizing a non-adversarial approach to problem solving may help resolve family legal issues with the least negative impact on the child or family in distress.[303]

Guardian *Ad Litem* Process

Role of the Social Worker

Generally, the court has the power to appoint a guardian *ad litem* for a minor child, if the child is not represented by a legally authorized person in a civil action,[304] if the minor child's guardian fails to pursue a claim on behalf of the child, or if the guardian is disqualified to act on the minor child's behalf.[305] In many jurisdictions, the appointment of a guardian *ad litem* for a minor child is provided for by statute.[306] Some jurisdictions require that a court appoint a guardian *ad litem* for an unrepresented minor in any action.[307] In most, however, appointment of a guardian *ad litem* remains within the court's discretion.[308]

In some jurisdictions, the courts can only appoint a guardian *ad litem* if conflicts of interest exist between minor children and their guardians or next friends, as in child custody proceedings, child abuse or neglect actions, or paternity actions.[309] Finally, some courts have held that a guardian *ad litem* is usually not necessary when a minor child has been charged with a crime, unless there is a showing of prejudice to the minor child.[310]

A guardian *ad litem* is typically regarded as an officer or agent of the court and is, therefore, under the control of the court. The guardian *ad litem* is responsible for protecting the minor child's rights and best interests, and for making recommendations to the court on the minor's behalf.[311] Thus, a guardian *ad litem* must determine whether it is in the child's best interest to continue, to settle, or to dismiss the suit for which he or she is appointed. In many jurisdictions any person, including non-lawyers may be appointed to serve as a guardian *ad litem*.[312] Some states established mandatory training to qualify as a guardian *ad litem*,[313] and a few states specifically require that a guardian *ad litem* be an attorney.[314] However, because most states have delegated the implementation of guardian *ad litem* statutes to counties, a clear, national pattern for the appointment and role of guardians *ad litem* does not exist.[315]

Many states permit the appointment of a guardian *ad litem* in contested divorce proceedings, in which child custody, visitation, and support are at issue.[316] However, the state statutes pertaining to the appointment of guardians *ad litem* tend to be non-uniform and to provide little guidance on the proper role of the guardian *ad litem* in a given case. The circumstances in which children are entitled to guardians *ad litem* are often unclear in statute texts.

Currently, 21 states have statutes allowing a court to appoint a guardian *ad litem* in divorce-related cases. Those states are: Alabama, Alaska, Florida, Hawaii, Illinois, Indiana, Iowa, Maine, Massachusetts, Michigan, Minnesota, Missouri, Montana, New Jersey, New Mexico, North Dakota, Ohio, Rhode Island, Texas, Virginia, and Wisconsin.[317] Of the above listed states, Florida, Minnesota,

Missouri, and Virginia require the appointment of a guardian *ad litem* if there is evidence of abuse or neglect of a minor child.[318]

Twenty-four states and the District of Columbia have statutes allowing a court to appoint "counsel" or an "attorney" for a minor child in divorce-related proceedings. It is unclear from the statutes whether this is the same as a guardian *ad litem*, and whether the court has appointed the individual to act in the minor's best interest. Those states are: Alaska, Arizona, California, Colorado, Connecticut, Delaware, District of Columbia, Florida, Illinois, Indiana, Iowa, Kentucky, Louisiana, Maryland, Nebraska, Ohio, Oklahoma, Pennsylvania, Rhode Island, South Dakota, Texas, Utah, Vermont, Virginia, and Washington.[319] Of the above, only Louisiana requires a court to appoint counsel for a minor child if there is evidence of abuse or neglect of the child.[320]

Finally, 10 states—Alaska, Arizona, Florida, Illinois, Indiana, Iowa, Ohio, Rhode Island, Texas, and Virginia—allow the courts to choose whether to appoint a guardian *ad litem*, counsel, or both in divorce-related proceedings.[321] Social workers may take on various roles in conjunction with the appointment of a guardian *ad litem*. First, if a social worker provides treatment to a child, a social worker may have the ability to bring to the attention of the court that a guardian *ad litem* may be needed. Generally, it is within the discretion of the court to determine if a guardian *ad litem* is needed and parental consent for the appointment of a guardian *ad litem* is not required.[322]

Second, a social worker, as well as the guardian *ad litem*, may be called to testify in court concerning the best interest of the child.[323] For example, in *Copiah County Department of Human Services v. Linda D.*,[324] the Supreme Court of Mississippi held that social workers should be allowed, "to give their opinions regarding the 'best interest' of minors based upon their investigations and personal observations."[325] Thus, a social worker may also be called upon to make a recommendation to the court concerning such issues as child custody.[326]

Social workers may also serve as guardians *ad litem* in some jurisdictions. For example, in *Creel v. Cornacchione*,[327] a social worker was appointed guardian *ad litem* to investigate allegations of emotional and physical abuse of two minor children during a modification of child support hearing.[328] The social worker in the *Creel* case was then allowed to report her findings to the court.[329] However, if they are not independent, social workers may not be allowed to serve as guardians *ad litem* (e.g., the social worker represents the agency that files a dependency petition).[330] Social workers should consult with their attorneys to determine their states' applicable laws governing the appointment of a guardian *ad litem*.

Release of Clinical Records to the Guardian *Ad Litem*

The question of whether or not a guardian *ad litem* has the right to access a social worker's client records, concerning the minor child the guardian *ad litem* represents, is of significant concern to social workers. Social workers must be familiar with the many legal requirements regarding confidentiality of records, particularly when parents or guardians *ad litem* wish to access children's records. Because disclosure of client records to guardians *ad litem* may cause children to forego any further communications with otherwise-trusted professionals, it is crucial that social workers are informed of the legal requirements of disclosure concerning their client records.

Some factors to be considered when social workers receive requests from guardians *ad litem* for minor children's client records include:

- whether access to the record has been required in a court order;
- whether a court order specifies that separate consent from a parent is needed;
- the age of the child; and
- whether the child consented to treatment independently.

At least one court, in the case *Rulong v. Rulong*,[331] held that the records of a minor child's treatment by a social worker are privileged communications.[332] Because the treatment records were privileged, the court held that the minor's guardian *ad litem* was not entitled to receive the records.[333] Furthermore, the court found that none of the exceptions to the privilege non-disclosure rule existed.

The court noted that, under the state statute on privileged communication, a social worker could be required to disclose a privileged communication if information in the privileged communication indicates that a "clear and present danger" exists to the life or health of the client or another person.[334] Because the child had not given consent to the disclosure, and there was no evidence that the communication to the social worker indicated a clear and present danger to the child, the social worker was not required to disclose the privileged communication to the minor child's guardian *ad litem*.[335] As evidenced in *Rulong*, social workers should consult with their attorneys to determine their states' laws governing disclosure of privileged communications.[336]

Conclusion

It is helpful for social workers who work with children to have some understanding of the complex legal issues relating to children, their legal status, their familial relationships, and the court processes in which children may be involved. Because these clients may be particularly vulnerable, social workers involved in treating children and families need to be aware of the legal provisions—as they pertain to the rights of minor clients—in the states where they practice. Also, the rights of children parented by lesbian and gay couples are expanding rapidly; social workers need to stay abreast of current developments and advocate for children in such families to have the same familial rights as other children.

Social workers should be guided by the *NASW Code of Ethics*, as well as by applicable legal provisions, when making decisions about minor clients' legal matters. This law note and its appendices provide references to other materials to guide social workers in continued research in each area. This is one tool, among many, created to assist social workers, and their counsel, with the professional treatment of children and their families.

Appendices

The following five appendices—referenced in the text—compile and compare state laws regarding topics discussed in this law note.

Appendix A provides a state-by-state summary of applicable laws pertaining to a minor's ability to make medical and mental health treatment decisions. This is an initial reference resource, which would also require a discussion with the minor to confirm the facts and possible review of related documents and/or discussion with the parents or an attorney. In addition, consultation with a state licensing board may be necessary to confirm the interpretation of the law.

Appendix B provides a state-by-state summary of applicable laws pertaining to a minor's competency to testify in court. (Appendix C also provides current legislation in a number of states that serve to protect child witnesses in the courtroom.)

Appendix C provides a state-by-state summary of applicable laws pertaining to the appointment of a guardian *ad litem* in various legal proceedings. Appendix C also provides a summary of the relevant state statutes pertaining to the appointment of "counsel" to a minor child in contested divorce-related proceedings.

Appendix D provides a state-by-state summary of applicable laws for custody determinations, specifically pertaining to those states that permit joint custody determinations.

Appendix E provides a state-by-state summary of applicable laws for a noncustodial parent's access to his or her child's records.

Appendix A:

Minors' Ability to Make Medical Decisions

As a general rule, minors are presumed incapable of providing or withholding consent to medical and mental health treatment. However, legislatures and courts have created exceptions to a minor's inability to give informed consent.

All states provide that an emancipated minor may consent independently to treatment. Furthermore, minors in all states may give consent to treatment for a sexually transmitted disease without the consent of a parent. In 43 states and the District of Columbia, minors may give consent to treatment for drug and alcohol abuse, while 23 jurisdictions allow them to consent to mental health treatment. Finally, 16 states allow minors to consent to medical treatment in emergency situations.

Table A1 provides a state-by-state summary of the applicable laws for a minor's ability to make medical decisions. Column 2 lists the relevant state laws governing the age of majority for each state. Columns 3 and 4 list the relevant state laws governing a minor's ability to consent independently to treatment for a sexually transmitted disease, or to treatment of drug or alcohol abuse, respectively. Column 5 lists the relevant state laws governing a minor's ability to consent to mental health treatment. Column 6 lists the 16 state laws that provide that a minor may consent to medical procedures in an emergency. Finally, where no applicable state law provision was found, the column has been left empty. Language preceding the state law provision provides a summary of the relevant provision and is not direct language from the provision.

Table A1: *State-by-State Summary of the Applicable Laws for a Minor's Ability to Make Medical Decisions*

STATE	AGE OF MAJORITY	STD/HIV SERVICES	DRUG/ALCOHOL ABUSE TREATMENT	MENTAL HEALTH SERVICES	EMERGENCY SERVICES
Alabama	19 years. Ala. Code § 26-1-1	Minor may consent independently. Ala. Code § 22-8-6	Minor may consent independently. Ala. Code § 22-8-6	Any minor who is 14 years of age or older, or a high school graduate, or is married, or is divorced, or is pregnant, may consent independently. Ala. Code § 22-8-4	Minor may consent independently in an emergency. Ala. Code § 22-8-3

STATE	AGE OF MAJORITY	STD/HIV SERVICES	DRUG/ALCOHOL ABUSE TREATMENT	MENTAL HEALTH SERVICES	EMERGENCY SERVICES
Alaska	18 years or upon marriage. Alaska Stat. § 25.20.10	Minor may consent independently. Alaska Stat. § 25.20.025(a)(4)			
Arizona	18 years. Ariz. Rev. Stat. Ann. § 1-215	Minor may consent independently. Ariz. Rev. Stat. Ann. § 44-132.01	Minor may consent independently. Ariz. Rev. Stat. Ann. § 36-2024, 44-133.01		Written parental consent required for surgical procedures unless emergency. Ariz. Rev. Stat. Ann. § 36-2271, 44-132
Arkansas	18 years. Ark. Code Ann. § 9-25-101	Minor may consent independently. Treatment information may be disclosed to parent over the express objection of the minor. Ark. Code Ann. § 20-16-508	Minor may consent independently. Ark. Code Ann. § 20-9-602	Minor may consent independently. Ark. Code Ann. § 20-9-602.	
California	18 years. Cal. Fam. Code § 6501	Minor may consent independently. Treatment plan shall include parents unless determined to be inappropriate by physician. Cal. Fam. Code § 6929	Any minor who is 12 years of age or older may consent independently if attending professional determines minor is "mature enough to participate intelligently in the outpatient services or residential shelter services" and there is a "danger of serious physical or mental harm to self or to others without the treatment or minor is the alleged victim of incest or child abuse."…Treatment plan shall include parents unless determined to be inappropriate by physician. Cal. Fam. Code § 6924		

STATE	AGE OF MAJORITY	STD/HIV SERVICES	DRUG/ALCOHOL ABUSE TREATMENT	MENTAL HEALTH SERVICES	EMERGENCY SERVICES
Colorado	21 years. Colo. Rev. Stat. Ann. § 2-4-401	Minor may consent independently. Colo. Rev. Stat. Ann. § 25-4-402	Minor may consent independently. Colo. Rev. Stat. Ann. § 13-22-102	A minor must be 15 years of age or older to consent to mental health services. However, a "professional person" who is rendering mental health services to the minor may advise the minor's parents or legal guardian with our without the minor's consent. Colo. Rev. Stat. Ann. § 27-10-103	
Connecticut	18 years. Conn. Gen. Stat. Ann. § 1-1d	Only with the consent of the minor's parents unless obtaining parental consent would result in treatment being denied or if minor requests that parents not be informed. Conn. Gen. Stat. Ann. § 39a-592.	Minor may consent independently. Conn. Gen. Stat. Ann. § 17a-682	Minor may consent independently. Conn. Gen. Stat. Ann. § 19a-14c	
Delaware	18 years. Del. Code Ann. tit. 1, § 701	Minor may consent independently. Del. Code Ann. tit. 13, § 710	Minor may consent independently. Del. Code Ann. tit. 16, § 2210		Minor may consent in an emergency. Reasonable efforts shall be made to obtain parental consent. Del. Code Ann. tit. 13, § 707 (b)(5)(ii)

STATE	AGE OF MAJORITY	STD/HIV SERVICES	DRUG/ALCOHOL ABUSE TREATMENT	MENTAL HEALTH SERVICES	EMERGENCY SERVICES
District of Columbia	18 years. D.C. Code Ann. § 46-101	Minor may consent independently. Notice to parent regarding HIV/AIDS testing is permitted. 22 D.C. Mun. Regs. § 600.7; D.C. Code Ann. § 7-1605.	Minor may consent independently. 22 D.C. Mun. Regs. § 600.7	A minor of any age may consent independently for mental health treatment D.C. Mun. Regs., tit. 22 § 600.7	
Florida	18 years or upon marriage. Fla. Stat. Ann. § 743.01, 743.07	Minor may consent independently. Fla. Stat. Ann. § 384.30	Minor may consent independently. Fla. Stat. Ann. § 349.499	A minor under the age of 18 years old must receive express and informed consent from his/her guardian "unless minor is seeking outpatient crisis intervention services under 394.4784." *See* Fla. Stat. Ann. § 394-495(3)(a). Any minor 13 years of age or older may independently consent to receive outpatient diagnostic, therapy, evaluation, and counseling services. *See Fla. Stat. Ann.* § 394.4784.	Minor may consent independently in an emergency. Fla. Stat. Ann. § 743.064
Georgia	18 years. Ga. Code Ann. § 39-1-1	Minor may consent independently. Results may be disclosed to minor's parents at the physician's discretion. Ga. Code Ann. § 37-7-8	Minor may consent independently. Ga. Code Ann. § 37-7-8	Written parental consent is required for treatment, if the patient is 12 years or older and under the age of 18. Ga. Code Ann. § 37-3-20(a)	

STATE	AGE OF MAJORITY	STD/HIV SERVICES	DRUG/ALCOHOL ABUSE TREATMENT	MENTAL HEALTH SERVICES	EMERGENCY SERVICES
Hawaii	18 years. Haw. Rev. Stat. Ann. § 577-1	Minor may consent independently. Results may be disclosed to minor's parents at the physician's discretion. Haw. Rev. Stat. Ann. § 577A-2, 577A-3	Minor may consent independently. Haw. Rev. Stat. Ann. § 577-26		
Idaho	18 years. Idaho Code § 32-101	Minor may consent independently. Idaho Code § 39-4302, 39-4303	Minor may consent independently. Idaho Code § 39-307	No Idaho statute addresses this issue.	
Illinois	18 years. 750 Ill. Comp. Stat. Ann. 30/3-1	Minor may consent independently. 410 Ill. Comp. Stat. Ann. 210/4	Minor may consent independently. 410 Ill. Comp. Stat. Ann. 210/4	Any minor 12 years of age or older may consent independently only for outpatient services. Moreover, any minor under the age of 17 years of age is limited to only 5 counseling sessions that may last for approximately 45 minutes, unless the minor receives consent from their guardian. 405 Ill. Comp. Stat. Ann. 5/3-501	Minor may consent independently in an emergency. 410 Ill. Comp. Stat. Ann. 210/3
Indiana	18 years. Ind. Code Ann. § 1-1-4-5	Minor may consent independently. Ind. Code Ann. § 16-36-1-3	A minor may consent independently. Ind. Code Ann. § 12-23-12-1		

STATE	AGE OF MAJORITY	STD/HIV SERVICES	DRUG/ALCOHOL ABUSE TREATMENT	MENTAL HEALTH SERVICES	EMERGENCY SERVICES
Iowa	18 years or upon marriage. Iowa Code Ann. § 599.1	Minor may consent independently. HIV/AIDS test must be disclosed to minor's parents. Iowa Code Ann. § 139A.35, 141.A7(3)	Minor may consent independently. Iowa Code Ann. § 125.33	A parent or legal guardian may only consent to mental health treatment for a minor. Iowa Code Ann. § 229.2	
Kansas	18 years. Kan. Stat. Ann. § 38-101	Minor may consent independently. Kan. Stat. Ann § 65-2892	Minor may consent independently. Kan. Stat. Ann. § 65-2892a	A minor who is 14 years of age or older may consent independently. However, the head of the treatment facility must immediately notify the minor's legal guardian about the minor's admission to the treatment facility. Kan. Stat. Ann. § 59-2949(2)(B)	Minor may consent independently in an emergency. Kan. Stat. Ann. § 65-2891
Kentucky	18 years. Ky. Rev. Stat. Ann. § 2.015	Minor may consent independently. Ky. Rev. Stat. Ann. § 214.185	Minor may consent independently. Ky. Rev. Stat. Ann. § 214.185	A minor who is 16 years of age or older may consent independently. Ky. Rev. Stat. Ann. § 214.185(2)	
Louisiana	18 years. La. Civ. Code Ann. art. 29	Minor may consent independently. La. Civ. Code Ann. 40 art. 1095	Minor may consent independently. La. Civ. Code Ann. 40 art. 1095		

STATE	AGE OF MAJORITY	STD/HIV SERVICES	DRUG/ALCOHOL ABUSE TREATMENT	MENTAL HEALTH SERVICES	EMERGENCY SERVICES
Maine	18 years. Me. Rev. Stat. Ann. tit. 1 § 73	Minor may consent independently. Me. Rev. Stat. Ann. tit. 22 § 1502, 1823	Minor may consent independently. Me. Rev. Stat. Ann. tit. 22 § 1502, 1823	Minor may consent independently if the minor is (1) living independent of parental support, (2) married or once legally married, (3) a member of the armed forces, or (4) legally emancipated. Me. Rev. Stat. Ann. tit. 22 § 1503. **Note:** The statute does not list any age restriction.	
Maryland	18 years. Md. Code Ann., Art. 1, § 24	Minor may consent independently. Md. Code Ann., Health Gen., Art. 20, § 102(b)(3)	Minor may consent independently. Md. Code Ann., Health Gen., Art. 20 § 102(b)(1),(2)	Minor may consent independently, if delaying the treatment to obtain consent will adversely affect the mental health of the minor Md. Code Ann., Health Gen., Art. 20, § 102 (d). Applies to treatment by psychiatrist, psychologist or MH clinic.	
Massachusetts	18 years. Mass. Gen. Laws Ann. ch. 231, § 85P	Minor may consent independently. Mass. Gen. Laws Ann. ch. 111, § 117	Minor may consent independently. Mass. Gen. Laws Ann. ch. 112, § 12E		

STATE	AGE OF MAJORITY	STD/HIV SERVICES	DRUG/ALCOHOL ABUSE TREATMENT	MENTAL HEALTH SERVICES	EMERGENCY SERVICES
Michigan	18 years. Mich. Comp. Laws Ann. § 722.52	Minor may consent independently. Mich. Comp. Laws Ann. § 333.5127	Minor may consent independently. Mich. Comp. Laws ann. § 333.6121	A minor who is 14 years of age or older may consent independently. Mich. Comp. Laws Ann. § 30.1707(1)	
Minnesota	18 years. Minn. Stat. Ann. § 645.451 (Subd. 5)	Minor may consent independently. Minn. Stat. Ann. § 144.343 (Subd. 1)	Minor may consent independently. Minn. Stat. Ann § 144.343 (Subd. 1)	Any minor living and managing their own affairs separate from his or her parents or legal guardian(s) may consent independently. Minn. Stat. Ann. § 144.341	Minor may consent independently in an emergency. Minn. Stat. Ann. § 144.344
Mississippi	18 for medical consent purposes, 21 for other purposes. Miss. Code Ann. §§ 41-41-51, 1-3-27	Minor may consent independently. Miss. Code Ann. § 41-41-13	Minor may consent independently. Miss. Code Ann. § 41-41-14	Any minor who is 15 years of age or older may consent independently. Miss. Code Ann. § 41-31-14	Minor may consent independently in an emergency. Miss. Code Ann § 41-41-7
Missouri	18 years. Mo. Ann. Stat. §§ 431.055, 431.061	Minor may consent independently. Mo. Ann. Stat. § 431.061 (4)(b)	Minor may consent independently. Mo. Ann. Stat. § 431.061 (4)(c)	A minor's parent or legal guardian is the only individual that may consent to the minor's treatment. Mo. Ann. Stat. § 632.110	
Montana	18 years. Mont. Code Ann. § 41-1-101	Minor may consent independently. Results may be disclosed to minor's parents. Mont. Code Ann. §§ 41-1402 (2)(c), 41-1-403	Minor may consent independently. Information may be disclosed to the minor's parents. Mont. Code Ann. §§ 41-1-402 (2)(c), 41-1-403	A minor who is 16 years of age or older, may consent independently. Mont. Code Ann. § 53-21-112(2)	Minor may consent independently in an emergency if no parent is immediately available. Mont. Code Ann. § 41-1-402(d)

STATE	AGE OF MAJORITY	STD/HIV SERVICES	DRUG/ALCOHOL ABUSE TREATMENT	MENTAL HEALTH SERVICES	EMERGENCY SERVICES
Nebraska	19 years. Neb. Rev. Stat. Ann. § 43-2101	Minor may consent independently. Neb. Rev. Stat. Ann. § 71-504			
Nevada	18 years. Nev. Rev. Stat. Ann. § 129.010	Minor may consent independently. Nev. Rev. Stat. Ann. § 129.060	Minor may consent independently. Physician must make every reasonable effort to report the treatment to the minor's parents. Nev. Rev. Stat. Ann. § 129.050		Minor may consent independently in an emergency. Nev. Rev. Stat. Ann. § 129.030(1)(d)
New Hampshire	18 years. N.H. Rev. Stat. Ann. § 21-B:1	Minor may consent independently. Results of positive HIV/AIDS test may be disclosed to minor's parents. N.H. Rev. Stat. Ann. §§ 141-C:18.11, 141-F:7-111	Minor may consent independently. N.H. Rev. Stat. Ann. § 318-B:12a	No statute or regulation on this issue.	
New Jersey	18 years. N.J. Stat. Ann. § 19:17B-3	Minor may consent independently. Results may be disclosed to minor's parents. N.J. Stat. Ann. §§ 9:17A-4, 9:17A-5	Minor may consent independently. Information may be disclosed to the minor's parents. N.J. Stat. Ann. § 9:17A-4		
New Mexico	18 years. N.M. Stat. Ann. § 28-6-1	Minor may consent independently. N.M. Stat. Ann. § 24-1-9		Minor 14 and older may consent independently to Medicaid services. N.M. Admin. Code § 7.20.11.22	

STATE	AGE OF MAJORITY	STD/HIV SERVICES	DRUG/ALCOHOL ABUSE TREATMENT	MENTAL HEALTH SERVICES	EMERGENCY SERVICES
New York	18 years. N.Y. Dom. Rel. Law § 2	Minor may consent independently. N.C. Gen. Stat. § 90-21.5(a)(i)	Minor may consent independently. N.Y. Men. Hy. § 22.11	Any minor may consent independently conditioned upon the following factors: (1) "the minor is knowingly... seeking such services; and (2) [the services are] necessary to minor's well-being" and (3) no legal guardian is "reasonably" available for consent. N.Y. Men. Hy. § 33.21	Minor may consent independently in an emergency. N.Y. Pub. He. Law § 2504
North Carolina	18 years. N.C. Gen. Stat. § 48A-2	Minor may consent independently. N.C. Gen. Stat. § 90-21.5(a)(i)	Minor may consent independently. N.C. gen. Stat. § 90-21.5	Minor may consent independently to MH treatment by physician. N.C. Gen. Stat. § 90-21.5(a)(iv)	Minor may consent independently in an emergency. N.C. gen. Stat. § 90-21.5
North Dakota	18 years. N.D. Cent. Code § 14-10-02	Minor may consent independently. N.D. Cent. Code § 14-10-17	Minor may consent independently. N.D. Cent. Code § 14-10-17		Minor may consent independently in an emergency. N.D. Cent. Code § 14-10-17.1
Ohio	18 years. Ohio Rev. Code Ann. § 3109.01	Minor may consent independently. Ohio Rev. Code Ann. § 3709.241	Minor may consent independently. Ohio Rev. Code Ann. § 3719.012	A minor who is 14 years of age or older may consent independently for outpatient services. Moreover, the minor may only receive six sessions or thirty days of outpatient treatment without parental consent. Ohio Rev. Code Ann. § 5122.04	

STATE	AGE OF MAJORITY	STD/HIV SERVICES	DRUG/ALCOHOL ABUSE TREATMENT	MENTAL HEALTH SERVICES	EMERGENCY SERVICES
Oklahoma	18 years. Okla. Stat. Ann. tit. 15, § 13; Okla. Stat. Ann. tit. 63, § 2601	Minor may consent independently. Results may be disclosed to minor's parents. Okla. Stat. Ann. tit. 16, § 2602	Minor may consent independently. Information may be disclosed to the minor's parents. Okla. Stat. Ann. tit. 63, § 2602 (A)(3)	A minor who is 16 years of age or older may consent independently for inpatient treatment. Okla. Stat. ann. tit. 43A § 5-503	Minor may consent independently in an emergency. Physician may inform minor's parents. Okla. Stat. ann. tit. 63, § 2602 (A)(7)
Oregon	18 years. Or. Rev. Stat. § 109.510	Minor may consent independently. Or. Rev. Stat. § 109.610	Minor may consent independently. Physician shall involve the minor's parents. Or. Rev. Stat. § 109.675 (1),(2)	A minor who is 14 years of age or older may consent independently. Physician shall involve the minor's parents unless they refuse. Or. Rev. stat. § 109.675	
Pennsylvania	21 years. 1 Penn. Cons. Stat. ann. § 1991	Minor may consent independently. 35 Penn. Cons. Stat. ann. § 10103	Minor may consent independently. 71 Penn. Cons. Stat. Ann. § 1690.112	A minor who is 14 years of age or older may consent independently. 35 penn. Cons. Stat. Ann. § 10101.1	
Rhode Island	18 years. R.I. gen. Laws § 15-12-1	Minor may consent independently. R.I. Gen. Laws § 23-8-1.1	Parental consent required unless physician determines it to be deleterious to treatment. R.I. Gen. Laws §§ 14-5-3, 14-5-4		
South Carolina	18 years. S.C. Code Ann. § 20-7-30	Minor may consent independently. S.C. Stat. Ann. §§ 20-7-280, 20-7-290	Minor may consent independently. S.C. Stat. Ann. §§ 20-7-280, 20-7-290		

STATE	AGE OF MAJORITY	STD/HIV SERVICES	DRUG/ALCOHOL ABUSE TREATMENT	MENTAL HEALTH SERVICES	EMERGENCY SERVICES
South Dakota	18 years. S.D. Codified Laws § 26-1-1	Minor may consent independently. S.D. Codified Laws § 34-23-16	Minor may consent independently. S.D. Codified Laws § 34-20A-50		Minor may consent independently in an emergency. S.D. Codified Laws § 20-9-4.2
Tennessee	18 years. Tenn. Code Ann. § 1-3-113	Minor may consent independently. Tenn. Code Ann. § 68-10-104(c)	Minor may consent independently. Tenn. Code Ann. § 63-6-220		Minor may consent independently in an emergency. Tenn. Code Ann. § 63-6-222
Texas	18 years. Texas Civ. Prac. & Rem. Code Ann. § 129.001	Minor may consent independently. Texas Fam. Code § 32.003(a)(3)	Minor may consent independently. Texas Fam. Code § 32.003 (a)(5)	Any minor who is 16 years of age or older and lives separate from their legal guardian(s) (e.g., minor managing his or her own financial affairs), may consent independently. Texas Fam. Code §§ 32.003, 32.004	
Utah	18 years or upon marriage. Utah Code Ann. § 15-2-1	Minor may consent independently. Utah Code Ann. tit. 26, § 26-6-18			
Vermont	18 years. Vt. Stat. Ann. tit. 1, § 173	Minor may consent independently. Physician must notify parents if such treatment requires immediate hospitalization. Vt. Stat. Ann. tit. 18, § 4226 (a)(2), (b)	Minor may consent independently. Physician must notify parents if such treatment requires immediate hospitalization. Vt. Stat. Ann. tit. 18, § 4226		

STATE	AGE OF MAJORITY	STD/HIV SERVICES	DRUG/ALCOHOL ABUSE TREATMENT	MENTAL HEALTH SERVICES	EMERGENCY SERVICES
Virginia	18 years. Va. Code Ann. § 1-204	Minor may consent independently. Results may be disclosed to minor's parents. Va. Code Ann. §§ 54.1-2969(E)(1), 32.1-36.1(10)	Minor may consent independently. Va. Code Ann. § 54.1-2969(E)(3)	Minor may consent independently to outpatient mental health services (no age restriction). Va. Code Ann. § 54.1-2969(E)(4)	
Washington	18 years. Wash. Rev. Code Ann. § 26.28.010	Minor may consent independently. Wash. Rev. Code Ann. § 70.24.110	Minor may consent independently. Wash. Rev. Code Ann. § 70.96A.095	A minor who is 13 years of age or older may consent independently. Wash. Rev. Code Ann. § 71.34.500	
West Virginia	18 years. W. Va. Code Ann. § 2-3-1	Minor may consent independently. W. Va. Code Ann. § 16-4-10			
Wisconsin	18 years; 17 years in a criminal or civil investigation or prosecution. Wis. Stat. Ann. § 48.02	Minor may consent independently. Wis. Stat. Ann. § 252.11	Minor may consent independently. Parental consent required in four situations.	A minor who is 14 years or older may consent to treatment, but must be accompanied with parental consent. Wis. Stat. Ann. § 51.61(6)	
Wyoming	18 years. Wyo. Stat. Ann. § 14-1-101	Minor may consent independently. Wyo. Stat. Ann. § 35-4-131			

Appendix B:

Minors' Competency to Testify

The legal system requires all witnesses who testify in court to be competent. However, under federal and most state laws, all witnesses are presumed to be competent, even young children. Thus, a court may determine a child's competency to testify on a case-by-case basis. A few states retain general prohibitions against child testimony, while allowing testimony in certain circumstances, such as in cases of child sexual abuse.

Many states have passed legislation to protect child witnesses in the courtroom. For example, some courts allow children's previous out-of-court statements to be admitted into evidence, while others allow children's previously videotaped statements to be admitted into evidence.

Table B1 provides a state-by-state summary of the applicable laws for minors' competency to testify. In addition to state laws governing children's competency, the following chart also lists statutes that provide protection to child witnesses in the courtroom. Column 2 lists the relevant state statute provisions or case law governing children's competency to testify and protections provided to child witnesses. Column 3 provides a summary of each state law provision listed but does not provide direct language from the statutes or case law.

Table B1 was prepared as of February 2006. For information subsequent to this date, interested parties should refer to the specific statutes or regulations or may contact their state social work boards regarding current statutes and regulations.

Table B1:   State-by-State Summary of the Applicable Laws for Minors' Competency to Testify

STATE	RELEVANT STATUTE	SUMMARY OF STATUTE
Alabama	Ala. Code § 12-21-165	Children who do not understand the nature of an oath are incompetent to testify.
Arizona	Ariz. Rev. Stat. Ann. § 12-2202	In a civil proceeding, children under age 10 who are incapable of receiving just impressions of the facts respecting which they are to testify are incompetent to testify.
	Ariz. Rev. Stat. Ann. § 13-4061	Every person is competent to testify in a criminal trial.
Arkansas	Ark. R. Evid. R. 601	Every person is competent to testify.
	Ark. Code Ann. § 16-44-203	Videotaped statement of child under age 17 who is an alleged victim of a sexual offense may be admissible.

Table B1: *State-by-State Summary of the Applicable Laws for Minors' Competency to Testify* (continued)

STATE	RELEVANT STATUTE	SUMMARY OF STATUTE
California	Cal. Evid. Code § 700, 701	Every person, irrespective of age, is competent to testify unless the person is incapable of expressing himself or understanding the duty to tell the truth.
Colorado	Colo. Rev. Stat. Ann. § 13-90-106	Children under 10 who are incapable of receiving just impressions of the facts respecting which they are examined are competent to testify.
	Colo. Rev. Stat. Ann. § 13-25-129	Hearsay statement of a child under age 15 who is an alleged victim of a sexual offense may be admissible.
	Colo. Rev. Stat. Ann. § 18-3-413	Videotaped statement of a child under age 15 who is an alleged victim of a sexual offense may be admissible.
Delaware	Del. Code Ann. § 4302	No child under age 10 may be excluded from testifying for the sole reason that the child doesn't understand the obligation of oath.
	Del. R. Evid. R. 601	Every person is competent to testify.
Florida	Fla. Stat. Ann. § 90.601, 90.602	Every person is competent to testify.
	Fla. Stat. Ann. § 90.605	Child may testify without taking oath if child understand the duty to tell the truth.
Georgia	Ga. Code Ann. § 24-9-1	Every person is competent to testify.
	Ga. Code Ann. § 24-9-5	Children that don't understand the oath are not competent, except in case of child molestation any child is competent.
	Ga. Code Ann. § 24-9-7	Court determines competency.
	Ga. Code Ann. § 24-3-16	Hearsay statement of child under age 14 describing sexual contact or physical abuse may be admissible.
Illinois	725 Ill. Comp. Stat. Ann. 5/115-14	Every person is competent to testify unless the person is incapable of expressing himself or understanding the duty to tell the truth.
Indiana	Ind. Code Ann. § 34-45-2-1, 35-37-4-1	Every person is competent to testify.
	Ind. Code Ann. § 35-37-4-6	Videotaped statement of child under age 14 is admissible.

STATE	RELEVANT STATUTE	SUMMARY OF STATUTE
Iowa	Iowa R. Evid. R. 5.601	Every person is competent to testify unless otherwise provided by statute.
Kansas	Kan Stat. Ann § 60-417	Person is disqualified as a witness if incapable of expressing himself or understanding the duty to tell the truth.
Louisiana	La. Civ. Code Ann. art. 13:3665	Competent witness is a person of proper understanding.
	Watermeier v. Watermeier	No precise age.
	La. Civ. Code Ann. art. 115	Child witness need not be placed under oath if the court can assure that child understands the duty to speak the truth.
Maryland	Md. Code Ann. art. 9 § 103	In criminal trial, age of child may not preclude child from testifying.
	Md. R. Evid. R. 6-601	Every person is competent to testify.
Massachusetts	Mass. Gen. Laws Ann ch. 233 § 20	Any person of sufficient understanding may testify.
	Com. V. Monzon 744 N.E. 2d 1131 (Mass Ct. App. 2001)	Two-prong test of competency: ability to observe and remember and understanding of difference between truth and falsehood.
Michigan	Mich. Comp. Laws Ann. § 600.2163a	For child under age 16: Video-taped statement of child may be permitted. Use of anatomically explicit dolls may be permitted to aid witness in testifying. Support person may be permitted to accompany witness during testimony.
	Mich. R. Evid. R. 600.1	Every person is competent to testify unless the person lacks capacity to understand the obligation to testify truthfully and understandably.
Missouri	Mo. Ann. Stat. § 491.060	Child under 10 years of age is incompetent to testify except a child under 10 who is alleged victim of a crime against the person, sexual offense, or crime against the family is a competent witness.

STATE	RELEVANT STATUTE	SUMMARY OF STATUTE
Montana	Mont. R. Evid. R. 601	Every person is competent to testify unless the person is incapable of expressing himself or understanding the duty to tell the truth.
	Mont. Cod Ann. § 46-16-220	Hearsay statement may be admissible for child who is an alleged victim of a sexual offense or crime of violence.
Nebraska	Neb. Rev. Stat. Ann. § 29-1926	For child under 11: Videotaped statement of child may be permitted. Support person may be permitted to accompany witness during testimony. On camera ("in chambers") testimony of child may be permissible.
Nevada	Nev. R. Evid. R. 601	Every person is competent to testify unless the person is incapable of expressing himself or understanding the duty to tell the truth.
New Mexico	N.M. R. Evid. R. 11-601	Every person is competent to testify.
New York	N.Y. Crim. Pro. Law § 60.20	Every person of sufficient intelligence is competent to testify. A child over the age of 9 may testify under oath.
		Use of closed circuit television may be used during testimony of a child.
North Carolina	N.C. Gen. Stat. § 8C-1, § 601	Every person is competent to testify unless the person is incapable of expressing himself or understanding the duty to tell the truth.
Ohio	Ohio rev. Cod Ann. § 2317.01	Every person is competent to testify except a child under age 10 who is incapable of receiving just impressions of the facts and transactions of which he or she is examined is incompetent to testify.
Oklahoma	Okla. Stat. Ann. tit. 17 § 2601	Every person is competent to testify.
Pennsylvania	42 Penn. Cons. Stat. Ann. § 5911	Every person is competent to testify.
South Dakota	S.D. Codified Laws § 19-14-1	Every person is competent to testify.

STATE	RELEVANT STATUTE	SUMMARY OF STATUTE
Texas	Texas R. Evid. R. 601	Every person is competent to testify, except a child who does not possess sufficient intelligence to relate transactions with respect to which her or she is interrogated is not competent to testify.
	Texas Code of Criminal Procedure Art. 38.072	Hearsay statement of child under age 12 who is a child abuse victim may be admissible.
Utah	Utah Code Ann. § 76-5-411	Hearsay statement of child under age 14 who is an alleged victim of sexual abuse may be admissible.
		Every person is competent to testify.
Vermont	Vt. R. Evid R. 601	Every person is competent to testify unless the person is incapable of expressing himself or understanding the duty to tell the truth.
Washington	Wash. Rev. Code Ann. § 5.60.020	Every person of sound mind may testify.
	Wash. Rev. Code Ann. § 5.60.050	Those incapable of receiving just impressions respecting which they are examined are not competent to testify.
	Wash. Rev. Code Ann. § 9A.44.120	Hearsay statement of a child under age 10 who is an alleged victim of a sex offense or physical abuse may be admissible.
West Virginia	W. Va. R. Evid. R. 601	Every person is competent to testify.
Wisconsin	Wis. Stat. Ann. § 906.01	Every person is competent to testify.

Appendix C:

Appointment of Guardian *Ad Litem* Laws

Generally, the court has the power to appoint a guardian *ad litem* for a minor child if he or she is not represented by a legally authorized person in a civil action, if the minor child's guardian fails to pursue a claim on behalf of the child, or if the guardian is disqualified to act on the minor child's behalf. In many jurisdictions, the appointment of a guardian *ad litem* is provided for by statute, while a few jurisdictions require that a court appoint a guardian *ad litem* for an unrepresented minor in any action. For example, Kansas Statutes Annotated § 60-217(c) states, "The court shall appoint a guardian *ad litem* for a minor...not otherwise represented in an action."

However, in other jurisdictions the appointment of a guardian *ad litem* remains within the court's discretion. For example, Florida Statutes Annotated § 61.401 states, "Rif the court finds it is in the best interests of the child, the court may apoint a guardian *ad litem* to act as next friend of the child." In many jurisdictions, the court may only appoint a guardian *ad litem* when a conflict of interest exists between the minor child and his or her guardian or next friend, as in a child custody proceeding, child abuse or neglect action, or paternity action.

Twenty-one states permit the appointment of a guardian *ad litem* in contested divorce proceedings if child custody, visitation, and support are at issue. Furthermore, 24 states and the District of Columbia have statutes that allow a court to appoint "counsel" for a minor child in divorce-related proceedings. However, it is often unclear from the statute whether this is the same as a guardian *ad litem*.

Table C1 provides a state-by-state summary of the applicable laws for the appointment of a guardian *ad litem* in various legal proceedings. The vast majority of those statutes listed pertain to divorce-related child custody, visitation, or support proceedings. A few statutes pertain to the appointment of a guardian *ad litem* in any type of civil action. For example, New Hampshire Revised Statute Annotated, § 464-A:41, provides that in "any proceeding in any court" a court may appoint a "disinterested person to act as guardian *ad litem*." Column 2 lists the type of proceeding to which the relevant guardian *ad litem* statutes pertain. Column 3 describes whether the appointment of a guardian *ad litem* by the court is mandatory or discretionary in a given situation, and Column 4 provides the relevant state statute and text for the appointment of a guardian *ad litem*.

Table C2 provides a state-by-state summary of the relevant state statutes pertaining to the appointment of "counsel" to a minor child in contested divorce-related proceedings. Column 2 lists the type of proceeding to which the relevant statute pertains, and Column 3 describes whether the appointment of counsel by the court is mandatory or discretionary. Column 4 provides the relevant state statute and text for the appointment of counsel for a minor child.

These tables were prepared as of May 2006. Interested parties should refer to the full statutes or regulations or contact their state social work board for current statutes and regulations.

Table C1: *Appointment of Guardian* Ad Litem *Statutes*

STATE	TYPE OF PROCEEDING	MANDATORY OR DISCRETIONARY APPOINTMENT	STATUTE AND TEXT
Alabama	Divorce-related	Discretionary	ALA. CODE § 26-2A-52. Guardian *ad litem*. At any point in a proceeding a court may appoint a guardian *ad litem* to represent the interest of a minor or other person if the court determines that representation of the interest otherwise would be inadequate. If not precluded by conflict of interests, a guardian *ad litem* may be appointed to represent several persons or interests.
Alaska	Divorce-related	Discretionary	ALASKA STAT. § 25.24.310. *Representation of minor*. Instead of, or in addition to, appointment of an attorney under (a) of this section, the court may, upon the motion of either party or upon its own motion, appoint an attorney or other person or the office of public advocacy to provide guardian *ad litem* services to a child in any legal proceedings involving the child's welfare. The court shall require a guardian *ad litem* when, in the opinion of the court, representation of the child's best interests, to be distinguished from preferences, would serve the welfare of the child. The court in its order appointing a guardian *ad litem* shall limit the duration of the appointment of the guardian *ad litem* to the pendency of the legal proceedings affecting the child's interests, and shall outline the guardian *ad litem*'s responsibilities and limit the authority to those matters related to the guardian's effective representation of the child's best interests in the pending legal proceeding. The court shall make every reasonable effort to appoint a guardian *ad litem* from among persons in the community where the child's parents or the person having legal custody or guardianship of the child's person reside...
Arizona	Termination of parental rights	Mandatory	ARIZ. REV. STAT. ANN. § 8-535. Notice of initial hearing; waiver; guardian *ad litem*... On the motion of any party or on its own motion, the court shall appoint a guardian *ad litem* it determines that there are reasonable grounds to believe that a party to the proceeding is mentally incompetent or is otherwise in need of a guardian *ad litem*.
	Juvenile court: abuse/neglect	Mandatory	ARIZ. REV. STAT. ANN. § 8-221(I). Counsel right of juvenile, parent or guardian; waiver; appointment; reimbursement; guardian *ad litem*... In all juvenile court proceedings in which the dependency petition includes an allegation that the juvenile is abused or neglected, the court shall appoint a guardian *ad litem* to protect the juvenile's best interests. This guardian may be an attorney or a court appointed special advocate.

STATE	TYPE OF PROCEEDING	MANDATORY OR DISCRETIONARY APPOINTMENT	STATUTE AND TEXT
Florida	Divorce-related	Discretionary	FLA. STAT. ANN. § 61.401. Appointment of guardian *ad litem*. In an action for dissolution of marriage, modification, parental responsibility, custody, or visitation, if the court finds it is in the best interest of the child, the court may appoint a guardian *ad litem* to act as next friend of the child, investigator or evaluator, not as attorney or advocate. The court in its discretion may also appoint legal counsel for a child to act as attorney or advocate; however, the guardian and the legal counsel shall not be the same person...
	Divorce-related: abuse/ neglect	Mandatory	FLA. STAT. ANN. § 61.401. Appointment of guardian *ad litem*... In such actions which involve an allegation of child abuse, abandonment, or neglect as defined in s. 39.01, which allegation is verified and determined by the court to be well-founded, the court shall appoint a guardian *ad litem* for the child. The guardian *ad litem* shall be a party to any judicial proceeding from the date of the appointment until the date of discharge.
	Any action where the minor is not represented	Mandatory	FLA. R. CIV. P. RULE 1.210(B). Infants or Incompetent Persons. When an infant or incompetent person has a representative, such as a guardian or other like fiduciary, the representative may sue or defend on behalf of the infant or incompetent person. An infant or incompetent person who does not have duly appointed representative may sue by next friend or by a guardian *ad litem*. The court shall appoint a guardian *ad litem* for an infant or incompetent person not otherwise represented in an action or shall make such other order as it deems proper for the protection of the infant or incompetent person.
Hawaii	Divorce-related	Discretionary	HAW. REV. STAT. ANN. § 571-46. Criteria and procedure in awarding custody and visitation... The court may appoint a guardian *ad litem* to represent the interests of the child and may assess the reasonable fees and expenses of the guardian *ad litem* as costs of the action, payable in whole or in part by either or both parties as the circumstances may justify.
Illinois	Divorce-related	Discretionary	750 ILL. COMP. STAT. ANN. 5/506. Representation of child. Duties. In any proceedings involving the support, custody, visitation, education, parentage, property interest, or general welfare of a minor or dependent child, the court may, on its own motion or that of any party, appoint an attorney to serve in one of the following capacities to address the issues the court delineates: Guardian *ad litem*. The guardian *ad litem* shall testify or submit a written report to the court regarding his or her recommendations in accordance with the best interest of the child. The report shall be made available to all parties. The guardian *ad litem* may be called as a witness for purposes of cross-examination regarding the guardian *ad litem*'s report or recommendations. The guardian *ad litem* shall investigate the facts of the case and interview the child and the parties.

STATE	TYPE OF PROCEEDING	MANDATORY OR DISCRETIONARY APPOINTMENT	STATUTE AND TEXT
Indiana	Divorce-related	Discretionary	IND. CODE ANN. § 31-15-6-1. APPOINTMENT. SEC. 1. A court in a proceeding under this article may appoint for a child at any time: • a guardian *ad litem*; • a court appointed special advocate; • or both.
Iowa	Divorce-related	Discretionary	IOWA CODE ANN. § 598.12. Attorney or guardian *ad litem* for minor child—investigations. The court may appoint a guardian *ad litem* to represent the best interests of the minor child or children of the parties. Unless otherwise enlarged or circumscribed by a court or juvenile court having jurisdiction over the child or by operation of law, the duties of a guardian *ad litem* with respect to a child shall include all of the following: • Conducting general in-person interviews with the child, if the child's age is appropriate for the interview, and interviewing each parent, guardian, or other person having custody of the child, if authorized by the person's legal counsel. • Conducting interviews with the child, if the child's age is appropriate for the interview, prior to any court-ordered hearing. • Visiting the home, residence, or both home and residence of the child and any prospective home or residence of the child, including visiting the home or residence or prospective home or residence each time placement is changed. • Interviewing any person providing medical, mental health, social, educational, or other services to the child, prior to any court-ordered hearing. • Obtaining firsthand knowledge, if possible, of facts, circumstances, and parties involved in the matter in which the person is appointed guardian *ad litem*. • Attending any hearings in the matter in which the person is appointed guardian *ad litem*.
Kansas	Any action where the minor is not represented	Mandatory	KAN. STAT. ANN. § 60-217(C). Minors or incapacitate persons. Whenever a minor or incapacitated person has a representative, such as a general guardian, committee, conservator, or other like fiduciary, the representative may sue or defend on behalf of the minor or incapacitated person. If a minor or incapacitated person does not have a duly appointed representative the minor or incapacitated person may sue by the minor or incapacitated person's next friend or by a guardian *ad litem*. The court shall appoint a guardian *ad litem* for a minor or incapacitate person not otherwise represented in an action or shall make such other order as it deems proper for the protection of the minor or incapacitated person.

STATE	TYPE OF PROCEEDING	MANDATORY OR DISCRETIONARY APPOINTMENT	STATUTE AND TEXT
Maine	Divorce-related	Discretionary	ME. REV. STAT. ANN. TIT. 19-A, § 1507. Appointment of guardian *ad litem* in contested proceedings. Guardian *ad litem*; appointment. In contested proceedings under sections 904 and 1653 in which a minor child is involved, the court may appoint a guardian *ad litem* for the child. The appointment may he made at any time, but the court shall make every effort to make the appointment as soon as possible after the commencement of the proceeding. The court may appoint a guardian *ad litem* when the court has reason for special concern as to the welfare of a minor child. In determining whether an appointment must he made, the court shall consider: • The wishes of the parties; • The age of the child; • The nature of the proceeding, including the contentiousness of the hearing; • The financial resources of the parties; • The extent to which a guardian *ad litem* may assist in providing information concerning the best interest of the child; • Whether the family has experienced a history of domestic abuse; • Abuse of the child by one of the parties; and • Other factors the court determines relevant. At the time of the appointment, the court shall specify the guardian *ad litem*'s length of appointment, duties, and fee arrangements.
Massachu-setts	Divorce-related	Discretionary	MASS. GEN. LAWS ANN. CH. 215, § 56A. INVESTIGATIONS. Any judge of a probate court may appoint a guardian *ad litem* to investigate the facts of any proceeding pending in said court relating to or involving questions as to the care. custody or maintenance of minor children and as to any matter involving domestic relations except those for the investigation of which provision is made by section 16 of chapter 208. Said guardian *ad litem* shall, before final judgment or decree in such proceeding, report in writing to the court the results of the investigation, and such report shall be open to inspection to all the parties in such proceeding or their attorneys. The compensation shall be fixed by the court and shall be paid by the commonwealth, together with an expense approved by the court, upon certificate by the judge to the state treasurer. The state police, local police, and probation officers shall assist the guardian *ad litem* so appointed, upon his or her request.

STATE	TYPE OF PROCEEDING	MANDATORY OR DISCRETIONARY APPOINTMENT	STATUTE AND TEXT
Michigan	Divorce-related	Discretionary	MICH. COMP. LAWS ANN. § 722.27(1)(D). Custody and support awards; parenting time; modification or amendment of judgments and orders; grandparenting time; other actions by court. Sec. 7. If a child custody dispute has been submitted to the circuit court as an original action under this act or has arisen incidentally from another action in the circuit court or an order or judgment of the circuit court, for the best interests of the child the court may do 1 or more of the following: ... Utilize a guardian *ad litem* or the community resources in behavioral sciences and other professions in the investigation and study of custody disputes and consider their recommendations for the resolution of the disputes.
	Where the minor does not have a conservator to represent him or her	Mandatory	MICH. COURT RULES RULE 2.201(E). Minors and Incompetent Persons. (1)... (c) If the minor or incompetent person does not have a conservator to represent the person as defendant, the action may not proceed until the court appoints a guardian *ad litem*, who is not responsible for the costs of the action unless, by reason of personal misconduct, he or she is specifically charged costs by the court. It is unnecessary to appoint a representative for a minor accused of a civil infraction. (2) *Appointment of Representative.* (a) Appointment of a next friend or guardian *ad litem* shall be made by the court as follows: • If the party is a minor 14 years of age or older, on the minor's nomination, accompanied by a written consent of the person to be appointed; • If the party is a minor under 14 years of age or an incompetent person, on the nomination of the party's next of kin or of another relative or friend the court deems suitable, accompanied by a written consent of the person to be appointed; or • If a nomination is not made or approved within 21 days after service of process, on motion of the court or of a party...
Minnesota	Divorce-related	Discretionary	MINN. STAT. ANN. § 518.165. Guardians for minor children. Subdivision 1. Permissive appointment of guardian *ad litem.* In all proceedings for child custody or for dissolution or legal separation where custody or parenting time with a minor child is in issue, the court may appoint a guardian *ad litem* from a panel established by the court to represent the interests of the child. The guardian *ad litem* shall advise the court with respect to custody, support, and parenting time.

STATE	TYPE OF PROCEEDING	MANDATORY OR DISCRETIONARY APPOINTMENT	STATUTE AND TEXT
Minnesota (continued)	Divorce-related: abuse/ neglect	Mandatory	MINN. STAT. ANN. § 518.165. Guardians for minor children. Subdivision 2. Required appointment of guardian *ad litem*. In all proceedings for child custody or for marriage dissolution or legal separation in which custody or parenting time with a minor child is an issue, if the court has reason to believe that the minor child is a victim of domestic child abuse or neglect, as those terms are defined in sections 260C.007 and 626.556, respectively, the court shall appoint a guardian *ad litem*. The guardian *ad litem* shall represent the interests of the child and advise the court with respect to custody, support, and parenting time. If the child is represented by a guardian *ad litem* in any other pending proceeding, the court may appoint that guardian to represent the child in the custody or parenting time proceeding. No guardian *ad litem* need be appointed if the alleged domestic child abuse or neglect is before the court on a juvenile dependency and neglect petition. Nothing in this subdivision requires the court to appoint a guardian *ad litem* in any proceeding for child custody, marriage dissolution, or legal separation in which an allegation of domestic child abuse or neglect has not been made.

	Any action where the minor is not represented	Mandatory	MINN. R. CIV. P. RULE 17.02.
			    Infants or Incompetent Persons. Whenever a party to an action is an infant or incompetent and has a representative duly appointed under the laws of this state or the laws of a foreign state or country. The representative may sue or defend on behalf of such party. A party who is an infant or is incompetent and is not so represented shall be represented by a guardian *ad litem* appointed by the court in which the action is pending or is to be brought. The guardian *ad litem* shall be a resident of this state, shall file a consent and oath with the court administrator, and shall give such bond as the court may require. A guardian *ad litem* appointed under this Rule is not a guardian *ad litem* within the meaning of the Rules of Guardian *Ad Litem* Procedure in Juvenile and Family Court and is not governed by those Rules except when appointed in a paternity action.
			    Any person, including an infant party over the age of 14 years and under no legal disability, may apply under oath for the appointment of a guardian *ad litem*. The application of the party or the party's spouse or parents or testamentary or other guardian shall have priority over other applications. If no such appointment is made on behalf of a defendant party before answer or default, the adverse party or a party's attorney may apply for such appointment, and in such case the court shall allow the guardian *ad litem* a reasonable time to respond to the complaint. ...

STATE	TYPE OF PROCEEDING	MANDATORY OR DISCRETIONARY APPOINTMENT	STATUTE AND TEXT
Missouri	Divorce-related	Discretionary	Mo. Ann. Stat. § 452.423. Guardian *ad litem* appointed, when, duties–fees–volunteer advocates, expenses. I. In all proceedings for child custody or for dissolution of marriage or legal separation where custody, visitation, or support of a child is a contested issue, the court may appoint a guardian *ad litem*.... The guardian *ad litem* shall: • Be the legal representative of the child at the hearing, and my examine, crosee-examine, subpoena witness and offer testimony; • Prior to the hearing, conduct all necessary interviews with persons having contact with or knowledge of the child in order to ascertain the child's wishes, feelings, attachments, and attitudes. If appropriate, the child should be interviewed; • Request the juvenile officer to cause a petition to be filed in the juvenile division of the circuit court if the guardian *ad litem* believes the child alleged to be abused or neglected is in danger....
	Divorce-related: abuse/neglect	Mandatory	Mo. Ann. Stat. § 452.423. Guardian *ad litem* appointed, when, duties—fees—volunteer advocates, expenses… The court shall appoint a guardian *ad litem* in any proceeding in which child abuse or neglect is alleged.

STATE	TYPE OF PROCEEDING	MANDATORY OR DISCRETIONARY APPOINTMENT	STATUTE AND TEXT
Montana	Divorce-related	Discretionary	MONT. CODE ANN. § 40-4-205. GUARDIAN *ad litem*. The court may appoint a guardian *ad litem* to represent the interests of a minor dependent child with respect to the child's support, parenting, and parental contact. The guardian *ad litem* may be an attorney. The county attorney, a deputy county attorney, if any, or the Department of Public Health and Human Services or any of its staff may not be appointed for this purpose. The guardian *ad litem* has the following general duties: • To conduct investigations that the guardian *ad litem* considers necessary to ascertain the facts related to the child's support, parenting, and parental contact; • To interview or observe the child who is the subject of the proceeding; • To make written reports to the court concerning the child's support, parenting, and parental contact; • To appear and participate in all proceedings to the degree necessary to adequately represent the child and make recommendation to the court concerning the child's support, parenting, and parental contact; • To perform other duties as directed by the court. The guardian *ad litem* has access to court, medical, psychological, law enforcement, social services, and school records pertaining to the child and the child's siblings and parents or caretakers. The court shall enter an order for costs and fees in favor of the child's guardian *ad litem*. The order must be made against either or both parents, except that if the responsible party is indigent, the costs must be waived.
New Hampshire	Any proceeding	Discretionary	N.H. REV. STAT. ANN. § 464-A:41 APPOINTMENT OF GUARDIANS *Ad Litem*. When before or during the hearing on any proceeding in any court it appears to the court that the interest or rights of a legally incapacitated person by age or other cause or circumstance are not fully represented or upon the request of any interested person, the court may appoint a competent and disinterested person to act as guardian *ad litem* for such legally incapacitated person and to represent such person's interest in the case. The guardian *ad litem* shall have none of the rights of the general guardian. The person appointed guardian *ad litem* shall make oath to perform such duty faithfully and impartially. A bond may be required of the guardian *ad litem* at the discretion of the court.

STATE	TYPE OF PROCEEDING	MANDATORY OR DISCRETIONARY APPOINTMENT	STATUTE AND TEXT
New Jersey	Divorce-related	Discretionary	N.J. Stat. Ann. § 9:2-4(c). Legislative findings and declarations; parents' right to custody equal; custody order; factors; guardian *ad litem*; agreement as to custody.... The court, for good cause and upon its own motion, may appoint a guardian *ad litem* or an attorney or both to represent the minor child's interests. The court shall have the authority to award a counsel fee to the guardian *ad litem* and the attorney and to assess that cost between the parties to the litigation.
New Mexico	Divorce-related	Discretionary	N.M. Stat. Ann. § 40-4-8. Contested custody; appointment of guardian *ad litem*. A. In any proceeding for the disposition of children when custody of minor children is contested by any party, the court may appoint an attorney at law as guardian *ad litem* on the court's motion or upon application of any party to appear for and represent the minor children. Expenses, costs and attorneys' fees for the guardian *ad litem* may be allocated among the parties as determined by the court.
North Dakota	Divorce-related	Discretionary	N.D. Cent. Code § 14-09-06.4. Appointment of guardian *ad litem* or child custody investigator for children in custody, support, and visitation proceedings—Immunity. In any action for an annulment, divorce, legal separation, or other action affecting marriage, when either party has reason for special concern as to the future of the minor children, and in any action when the custody or visitation of children is contested, either party to the action may petition the court for the appointment of a guardian *ad litem* to represent the children concerning custody, support, and visitation. The court, in its discretion, may appoint a guardian *ad litem* or child custody investigator on its own motion. If appointed, a guardian *ad litem* shall serve as an advocate of the children's best interests. If appointed, the child custody investigator shall provide those services as prescribed by the supreme court. The court may direct either or both parties to pay the guardian *ad litem* or child custody investigator fee established by the court. If neither party is able to pay the fee, the court may direct the fee to he paid, in whole or in part, by the county of venue. The court may direct either or both parties to reimburse the county, in whole or in part, for such payment. Any guardian *ad litem* or child custody investigator appointed under this section who acts in good faith in making a report to the court is immune from any civil liability resulting from the report. For the purpose of determining good faith, the good faith of the guardian *ad litem* or child custody investigator is a disputable presumption.
	To enforce the minor's rights	Mandatory	N.D. Cent. Code § 14-10-04. Minor's rights of action. A minor may enforce the minor's rights by civil action or other legal proceedings in the same manner as an adult, except that a guardian *ad litem* must he appointed to conduct the same.

STATE	TYPE OF PROCEEDING	MANDATORY OR DISCRETIONARY APPOINTMENT	STATUTE AND TEXT
Ohio	Divorce-related	Discretionary	OHIO R. CIV. P. 75(B)(2). Divorce, annulment, and legal separation actions… When it is essential to protect the interests of a child, the court may join the child of the parties as a party defendant and appoint a guardian *ad litem* and legal counsel, if necessary, for the child and tax the costs….
Rhode Island	Divorce-related	Discretionary	R.I. GEN. LAWS § 15-5-16.2(C). Child support. The court may, if in its discretion it deems it necessary or advisable, appoint an attorney or a guardian *ad litem* to represent the interest of a minor or dependent child with respect to his or her support, custody, and visitation.
Tennessee	Any juvenile proceeding	Mandatory	TENN. R. JUV. P. 37. § 37-1-149. *Guardian ad litem—Special advocate.* The court at any stage of a proceeding under this part, on application of a party or on its own motion, shall appoint a guardian *ad litem* for a child who is a party to the proceeding if such child has no parent, guardian or custodian appearing on such child's behalf or such parent's, guardian's or custodian's interests conflict with the child's or in any other case in which the interests of the child require a guardian. The court, in any proceeding under this part resulting from a report of harm or an investigation report under § § 37-1-401 – 37-1-411, shall appoint a guardian *ad litem* for the child who was the subject of the report. A party to the proceeding or the party's employee or representative shall not be appointed.
Texas	Divorce-related	Discretionary	TEX. FAM. CODE ANN. § 107.001/ DEFINITIONS… "Guardian *ad litem*" means a person appointed to represent the best interests of a child. The term includes: • A volunteer advocate appointed under Subchapter C; • A professional, other than an attorney, who holds a relevant professional license, and whose training relates to the determination of a child's best interests; • An adult having the competence, training, and expertise determined by the court to be sufficient to represent the best interests of the child; or • An attorney *ad litem* appointed to serve in the dual role.

STATE	TYPE OF PROCEEDING	MANDATORY OR DISCRETIONARY APPOINTMENT	STATUTE AND TEXT
Virginia	Divorce-related	Discretionary	VA. CODE ANN. § 16.1-266. Appointment of counsel and guardian *ad litem*... F. In all other cases which in the discretion of the court require counsel or a guardian *ad litem*, or both, to represent the child or children or the parent or guardian, discreet and competent attorneys-at-law may be appointed by the court. However, in cases where the custody of a child or children is the subject of controversy or requires determination and each of the parents or other persons claiming a right to custody is represented by counsel, the court shall not appoint counsel or a guardian *ad litem* to represent the interests of the child or children unless the court finds, at any stage in the proceedings in a specific case, that the interests of the child or children are not otherwise adequately represented.
	Divorce-related: abuse/neglect	Mandatory	VA. CODE ANN. § 16.1-266. Appointment of counsel and guardian *ad litem*. A. Prior to the hearing by the court of any case involving a child who is alleged to be abused or neglected or who is the subject of an entrustment agreement or a petition seeking termination of residual parental rights or who is otherwise before the court pursuant to subdivision A4 of § 6.1-241 or § 63.2-1230, the court shall appoint a discreet and competent attorney-at-law as guardian *ad litem* to represent the child pursuant to § 16.1-266.1.

STATE	TYPE OF PROCEEDING	MANDATORY OR DISCRETIONARY APPOINTMENT	STATUTE AND TEXT
Wisconsin	Divorce-related	Mandatory	WIS. STAT. ANN. § 767.045. Guardian *ad litem* for minor children. *Appointment.* The court shall appoint a guardian *ad litem* for a minor child in any action affecting the family if any of the following conditions exists: • The court has reason for special concern as to the welfare of a minor child. • ...the legal custody or physical placement of the child is contested. The court may appoint a guardian *ad litem* for a minor child in any action affecting the family if the child's legal custody or physical placement is stipulated to be with any person or agency other than a parent of the child or, if at the time of the action, the child is in the legal custody of, or physically placed with, any person or agency other than the child's parent by prior order or by stipulation in this or any other action.... *Responsibilities.* The guardian *ad litem* shall be an advocate for the best interests of a minor child as to paternity, legal custody, physical placement, and support. The guardian *ad litem* shall function independently, in the same manner as an attorney for a party to the action, and shall consider, but shall not be bound by, the wishes of the minor child or the positions of others as to the best interests of the minor child. The guardian *ad litem* shall consider the factors under s.767.24(5)(am), subject to s. 767.24(5)(bm), and custody studies under s. 767.11(14). The guardian *ad litem* shall investigate whether there is evidence that either parent has engaged in interspousal battery, as described in s. 940.19 or 940.20(1m), or domestic abuse, as defined in s. 813.12(1)(am), and shall report to the court on the results of the investigation. The guardian *ad litem* shall review and comment to the court on any mediation agreement and stipulation made under s. 767.11(12) and on any parenting plan filed under s. 767.24(1m). Unless the child otherwise requests, the guardian *ad litem* shall communicate to the court the wishes of the child as to the child's legal custody or physical placement under s. 767.24(5)(am)2. The guardian *ad litem* has none of the rights or duties of a general guardian.

STATE	TYPE OF PROCEEDING	MANDATORY OR DISCRETIONARY APPOINTMENT	STATUTE AND TEXT
Wisconsin (continued)	Any action where the minor is not represented	Mandatory	WIS. STAT. ANN. § 803.01(3). INFANTS OR INCOMPETENT PERSONS. *Appearance by guardian or guardian ad litem.* If a party to an action or proceeding is a minor, or if the court has reason to believe that a party is mentally incompetent to have charge of the party's affairs, the party shall appear by an attorney, by the general guardian of the party's property who may appear by attorney or by a guardian *ad litem* who may appear by an attorney. A guardian *ad litem* shall be appointed in all cases where the minor or incompetent has no general guardian of property, or where the general guardian fails to appear and act on behalf of the ward or incompetent, or where the interest of the minor or incompetent is adverse to that of the general guardian. Except as provided in s. 807.10, if the general guardian does appear and act and the interests of the general guardian are not adverse to the minor or incompetent, a guardian *ad litem* shall not be appointed. Except as provided in s. 879.23(4), where the interests of the minor or mentally incompetent person are represented by an attorney of record the court shall, except upon good cause stated in the record, appoint that attorney as the guardian *ad litem*. *Guardian ad litem.* The guardian *ad litem* shall be appointed by a circuit court of the county where the action is to be commenced or is pending, except that the guardian *ad litem* shall he appointed by a circuit court commissioner of the county in actions to establish paternity that are before the circuit court commissioner. When the plaintiff is a minor 14 years of age or over, upon the plaintiffs application or upon the state's application under s. 767.045(1)(c); or if the plaintiff is under that age or is mentally incompetent, upon application of the plaintiffs guardian or of a relative or friend or upon application of the state under s. 767.045(I)(c). If the application is made by a relative, friend or the state, notice thereof must first be given to the guardian if the plaintiff has one in this state; if the plaintiff has none, then to the person with whom the minor or mentally incompetent resides or who has the minor or mentally incompetent in custody. When the defendant is a minor 14 years of age or over, upon the defendant's application made within 20 days after the service of the summons or other original process; if the defendant is under that age or neglects to so apply or is mentally incompetent, then upon the court's own motion or upon the application of any other party or any relative or friend or the defendant's guardian upon such notice of the application as the court directs or approves....

Table C2: *Appointment of Counsel in Divorce-Related Proceedings*

STATE	MANDATORY OR DISCRETIONARY APPOINTMENT	STATUTE AND TEXT
Alaska	Discretionary	ALASKA STAT. § 25.24.310. Representation of minor. (a) In an action involving a question of the custody, support, or visitation of a child, the court may, upon the motion of a party to the action or upon its own motion, appoint an attorney or the office of public advocacy to represent a minor with respect to the custody, support, and visitation of the minor or in any other legal proceeding involving the minor's welfare or to represent an unmarried 18-year-old child with respect to post-majority support while the child is actively pursuing a high school diploma or an equivalent level of technical or vocational training and living as a dependent with a parent or guardian or a designee of the parent or guardian. When custody, support, or visitation is at issue in a divorce, it is the responsibility of the parties or their counsel to notify the court that such a matter is at issue. Upon notification, the court shall determine whether the minor or other child should have legal representation or other services and shall make a finding on the record before trial…
Arizona	Discretionary	ARIZ. REV. STAT. ANN. § 25-321. Representation of child by counsel; fees. The court may appoint an attorney to represent the interests of a minor or dependent child with respect to his support, custody and visitation. The court may enter an order for costs, fees and disbursements in favor of the child's attorney. The order may be made against either or both parents.
California	Discretionary	CAL. FAM. CODE § 3150. (a) If the court determines that it would be in the best interest of the minor child, the court may appoint private counsel to represent the interests of the child in a custody or visitation proceeding.
Colorado	Discretionary	COLO. REV. STAT. ANN. § 14-10-116. Appointment in domestic relations cases—representation of child's best interest—legal representative of the child. (1) The court may, upon the motion of either party or upon its own motion, appoint an attorney, in good standing and licensed to practice law in the state of Colorado, to serve as the legal representative of the child, representing the best interests of the child in any domestic relations proceeding that involves allocation of parental responsibilities.
Connecticut	Discretionary	CONN. GEN. STAT. ANN. § 46b-54. Counsel for minor children. Duties. (a) The court may appoint counsel for any minor child or children of either or both parties at any time after the return day of a complaint under section 46b-45, if the court deems it to be in thebest interests of the child or children. The court may appoint counsel on its own motion, or at the request of either of the parties or of the legal guardian of any child or at the request of any child who is of sufficient age and capable of making an intelligent request.
Delaware	Discretionary	DEL. CODE ANN. TIT. 13, § 721(c). Commencement of proceedings; venue; notice; pleadings; attorney for child; removal from jurisdiction; considerations… (c) The Court may, in the interest of the child, appoint an attorney to represent the child in the proceedings. A fee for an attorney so appointed shall be allowed as part of the costs of the proceeding.

STATE	MANDATORY OR DISCRETIONARY APPOINTMENT	STATUTE AND TEXT
District of Columbia	Discretionary	D.C. Code Ann. § 16-918(b). Appointment of counsel; compensation; termination of appointment… (b) In any proceeding wherein the custody of a child is in question, the court may appoint a disinterested attorney to appear on behalf of the child and represent his best interests.
Florida	Discretionary	Fla. Stat. Ann. § 61.401. Appointment of guardian *ad litem*. In an action for dissolution of marriage, modification, parental responsibility, custody, or visitation, if the court finds it is in the best interest of the child, the court may appoint a guardian *ad litem* to act as next friend of the child, investigator or evaluator, not as attorney or advocate. The court in its discretion may also appoint legal counsel for a child to act as attorney or advocate; however, the guardian and the legal counsel shall not be the same person. In such actions which involve an allegation of child abuse, abandonment, or neglect as defined in s. 39.01, which allegation is verified and determined by the court to be well-founded, the court shall appoint a guardian *ad litem* for the child. The guardian *ad litem* shall be a party to any judicial proceeding from the date of the appointment until the date of discharge.
Illinois	Discretionary	750 Ill. Comp. Stat. Ann. 5/506. Representation of child. (a) Duties. In any proceedings involving the support, custody, visitation, education, parentage, property interest, or general welfare of a minor or dependent child, the court may, on its own motion or that of any party, appoint an attorney to serve in one of the following capacities to address the issues the court delineates: (I) Attorney. The attorney shall provide independent legal counsel for the child and shall owe the same duties of undivided loyalty, confidentiality, and competent representation as are due an adult client… (3) Child representative. The child representative shall advocate what the child representative finds to the in the best interests of the child after reviewing the facts and circumstances of the case. The child representative shall meet with the child and the parties, investigate the facts of the case, and encourage settlement and the use of alternative forms of dispute resolution. The child representative shall have the same authority and obligation to participate in the litigation as does an attorney for a party and shall possess all the powers of investigation as does a guardian *ad litem*. The child representative shall consider, but not be bound by, the expressed wishes of the child. A child representative shall have received training in child advocacy or shall possess such experience as determined to be equivalent to such training by the chief judge of the circuit where the child representative has been appointed. The child representative shall not disclose confidential communications made by the child, except as required by law or by the Rules of Professional Conduct. The child representative shall not render an opinion, recommendation, or report to the court and shall not be called as a witness, but shall offer evidence-based legal arguments. The child representative shall disclose the position as to what the child representative intends to advocate in a pre-trial memorandum that shall be served upon all counsel of record prior to the trial. The position disclosed in the pre-trial memorandum shall not be considered evidence. The court and the parties may consider the position of the child representative for purposes of a settlement conference.

STATE	MANDATORY OR DISCRETIONARY APPOINTMENT	STATUTE AND TEXT
Indiana	Discretionary	IND. CODE ANN. § 31-15-6-1. Appointment. Sec. 1. A court in a proceeding under this article may appoint: (1) a guardian *ad litem*; (2) a court appointed special advocate; or (3) both; for a child at any time.
Iowa	Discretionary	IOWA CODE ANN. § 598.12. Attorney or guardian *ad litem* for minor child—investigations. 1. The court may appoint an attorney to represent the legal interests of the minor child or children of the parties. The attorney shall be empowered to make independent investigations and to cause witnesses to appear and testify before the court on matters pertinent to the legal interests of the children…
Kentucky	Discretionary	KY. REV. STAT. ANN. § 403.090. Friend of the court; appointment; tenure; duties; wage withholding collections; compensation. (1) The fiscal court of any county may, by resolution, authorize the appointment of a "friend of the court." … (4) In any action for divorce where the parties have minor children, the friend of the court, if requested by the trial judge, shall make such investigation as will enable the friend of the court to ascertain all facts and circumstances that will affect the rights and interests of the children and will enable the court to enter just and proper orders and judgment concerning the care, custody, and maintenance of the children. The friend of the court shall make a report to the trial judge, at a time fixed by the judge, setting forth recommendations as to the care, custody, and maintenance of the children. The friend of the court may request the court to postpone the final submission of any case to give the friend of the court a reasonable time in which to complete the investigation.
Louisiana	Discretionary	LA. REV. STAT. ANN. § 9:345. Appointment of attorney in child custody or visitation proceedings. A. In any child custody or visitation proceeding, the court, upon its own motion, upon motion of any parent or party, or upon motion of the child, may appoint an attorney to represent the child if, after a contradictory hearing, the court determines such appointment would be in the best interest of the child…
	Mandatory: abuse/neglect	B. The court shall appoint an attorney to represent the child if, in the contradictory hearing, any party presents a prima facie case that a parent or other person caring for the child has sexually, physically, or emotionally abused the child or knew or should have known that the child was being abused.
Maryland	Discretionary	MD. CODE ANN., FAM. LAW § 1-202. Appointment of counsel for minor. In an action in which custody, visitation rights, or the amount of support of a minor child is contested, the court may: (1) appoint to represent the minor child counsel who may not represent any party to the action; and (2) impose against either or both parents counsel fees.

STATE	MANDATORY OR DISCRETIONARY APPOINTMENT	STATUTE AND TEXT
Nebraska	Discretionary	NEB. REV. STAT. ANN. § 42-358(1). Attorney for minor child; appointment; powers; child or spousal support; records; income withholding; contempt proceedings; fees; evidence; appeal. (1) The court may appoint an attorney to protect the interests of any minor children of the parties. Such attorney shall be empowered to make independent investigations and to cause witnesses to appear and testify on matters pertinent to the welfare of the children.
Ohio	Discretionary	OHIO R. CIV. P. 75(B)(2). Divorce, annulment, and legal separation actions… (2) When it is essential to protect the interests of a child, the court may join the child of the parties as a party defendant and appoint a guardian *ad litem* and legal counsel, if necessary, for the child…

Oklahoma	Discretionary	OKLA. STAT. ANN. TIT. 10, § 24.
		  Appointment of counsel—Responsibilities of Oklahoma Indigent Defense System—Compensation. A. 1. When it appears to the court that a minor or the minor's parent or legal guardian desires counsel but is indigent and cannot for that reason employ counsel, the court shall appoint counsel.
		  2. In any case in which it appears to the court that there is a conflict of interest between a parent or legal guardian and a child so that one attorney could not properly represent both, the court may appoint counsel, in addition to counsel already employed by a parent or guardian or appointed by the court to represent the minor or parent or legal guardian; provided, that in all counties having county indigent defenders, the county indigent defenders assume the duties of representation in proceedings such as above.

Pennsylvania	Discretionary	PA. R. CIV. P. 1915.11. Appointment of Attorney for Child. Interrogation of Child. Attendance of Child at Hearing or Conference. (a) The court may on its own motion or the motion of a party appoint an attorney to represent the child in the action. The court may assess the cost upon the parties or any of them or as otherwise provided by law.
Rhode Island	Discretionary	R.I. GEN. LAWS § 15-5-16.2(c). Child support… (c) (I) The court may, if in its discretion it deems it necessary or advisable, appoint an attorney or a guardian *ad litem* to represent the interest of a minor or dependent child with respect to his or her support, custody, and visitation.
South Dakota	Discretionary: abuse/neglect Discretionary: parent/guardian requests appointment	S.D. CODIFIED LAWS § 25-4-45.4. Counsel appointed for child
Texas	Discretionary	TEX. FAM. CODE ANN. § 107.001. Definitions… (2) "Attorney *ad litem*" means an attorney who provides legal services to a person, including a child, and who owes to the person the duties of undivided loyalty, confidentiality, and competent representation.

STATE	MANDATORY OR DISCRETIONARY APPOINTMENT	STATUTE AND TEXT
Utah	Discretionary	UTAH CODE ANN. § 30-3-11.2. Appointment of counsel for child. If, in any action before any court of this state involving the custody or support of a child, it shall appear in the best interests of the child to have a separate exposition of the issues and personal representation for the child, the court may appoint counsel to represent the child throughout the action, and the attorney's fee for such representation may be taxed as a cost of the action.
Vermont	Discretionary	VT. STAT. ANN. TIT. 15, § 594. Representation and testimony of child. (a) The court may appoint an attorney to represent the interest of a minor or dependent child with respect to child support and the allocation of parental rights and responsibilities.
	Mandatory: child called as witness	VT. STAT. ANN. TIT. 15, § 594. § 594. Representation and testimony of child. ... (b) The court shall appoint an attorney for a minor child before the minor child is called as a witness in a proceeding under this chapter...

Virginia	Discretionary	VA. CODE ANN. § 16.1-266.
		    Appointment of counsel and guardian *ad litem*... F. In all other cases which in the discretion of the court require counsel or a guardian *ad litem*, or both, to represent the child or children or the parent or guardian, discreet and competent attorneys-at-law may he appointed by the court.
		    However, in cases where the custody of a child or children is the subject of controversy or requires determination and each of the parents or other persons claiming a right to custody is represented by counsel, the court shall not appoint counsel or a guardian *ad litem* to represent the interests of the child or children unless the court finds, at any stage in the proceedings in a specific case, that the interests of the child or children are not otherwise adequately represented.

Washington	Discretionary	WASH. REV. CODE ANN. § 26.09.110. Minor or dependent child—Court appointed attorney to represent—Payment of costs, fees, and disbursements. The court may appoint an attorney to represent the interests of a minor or dependent child with respect to provision for the parenting plan in an action for dissolution of marriage, legal separation, or declaration concerning the validity of a marriage. The court shall enter an order for costs, fees, and disbursements in favor of the child's attorney.

Appendix D:

Child Custody Laws

Generally, courts take into consideration all of the surrounding circumstances of each particular case when making custody determinations. Courts and legislatures have enumerated many factors to be considered in a custody decision, in order to determine the custody arrangement that is in the best interest of the child.

Some states have found that joint custody is usually in the best interest of the child, and allow a joint custody determination to be made. Hawaii Revised Statute § 571-46.1(a) states, "Upon the application of either parent, joint custody may be awarded in the discretion of the court." A minority of states created a rebuttable presumption that joint custody is in the best interest of the child. For example, District of Columbia Code 16-914(a)(2) states, "There shall be a rebuttable presumption that joint custody is in the best interests of the child or children."

The following chart provides a state-by-state summary of the applicable laws for custody determinations. Column 2 includes the relevant state statutes or case law that permit joint custody determinations. Column 3 provides the state statutes that include a rebuttable presumption for joint custody, and Column 4 outlines state statutes that enumerate the statutory factors used in custody determinations.

These tables were prepared as of May 2006. Interested parties should refer to the specific statutes or regulations or contact their state social work board for current statutes and regulations.

Table D1: *State-by-State Summary of the Applicable Laws for Custody Determinations*

STATE	COURT MAY AWARD JOINT CUSTODY	PRESUMPTION OF JOINT CUSTODY	STATUTORY GUIDELINES PROVIDED
Alabama	Ala. Code § 30-3-152(a) (court may award joint custody where it is in the best interest of the child).	Ala. Code § 30-3-152(c) (joint custody presumed where both parties consent).	Ala. Code § 30-3-152(a).
Alaska	Alaska Stat. § 25.20.060(c) (court may award shared custody if it is in the best interest of the child).		Alaska Stat. § 25.20.090.
Arizona	Ariz. Rev. Stat. Ann. § 25-402(C) (court may award joint custody if it is in the best interest of the child). Ariz. Rev. Stat. Ann. § 25402(C) (court may award joint legal custody without awarding joint physical custody).		Ariz. Rev. Stat. Ann. § 25-403(D).

Table D1: *State-by-State Summary of the Applicable Laws for Custody Determinations* (continued)

STATE	COURT MAY AWARD JOINT CUSTODY	PRESUMPTION OF JOINT CUSTODY	STATUTORY GUIDELINES PROVIDED
Arkansas	Ark. Code Ann. § 9-13-1 ()1(b)(1)(A)(ii) (court may award joint custody if it is in the best interest of the child).		No statute
California	Cal. Fam. Code § 3081 (court may award joint custody). Cal. Fam. Code § 3085 (court may award joint legal custody without awarding joint physical custody).	Cal. Fam. Code § 3080 (joint custody presumed only where both parties agree).	Cal. Fam, Code § 3011.
Colorado	Colo. Rev. Stat. Ann. § 14-10-124(1.5)(b) (court may award joint custody if it is in the best interest of the child).		Colo. Rev. Stat. Ann. § 14-10-124(1.5)(b).
Connecticut		Conn. Gen. Stat. Ann. § 46b-56a(b) (joint custody presumed where both parties agree).	Conn. Gen. Stat. Ann. § 46b-56(b).
Delaware	Del. Code Ann. tit. 13. § 728 (court may award joint custody if it is in the best interest of the child).		Del, Code Ann. tit. 13, § 722.
District of Columbia	D.C. Code Ann. § 16-9 1 4(a) (1)(A) (court may award joint custody).	D.C. Code Ann. § 16- 914(a)(2) (joint custody presumed except where there is evidence of child abuse or neglect).	D.C. Code Ann. § 16-914(03).
Florida		Ha. Stat. Ann. § 61.13(2)(h)(2) (presumption of shared parental responsibility unless it will be detrimental to the child).	Fla. Stat. Ann. § 61.13(3).
Georgia	Ga. Code Ann. § 19-9- 3(a)(5) (court may award joint custody).		Ga. Code Ann. § 19-9-1.
Hawaii	Haw. Rev. Stat. Ann. § 571-46.1(a) (court may award joint custody).		Haw. Rev. Stat. Ann. § 571-46.
Idaho		Idaho Code § 32-71713(4) (joint custody presumed)	Idaho Code § 32-717.
Illinois	750 Ill. Comp. Stat. Ann. 5/602.1(c) (court may award joint custody if it is in the best interest of the child).		750 Ill. Comp. Stat. Ann. 5/602.
Indiana	Ind. Code Ann. § 31-17-2- 13 (court may award joint custody if it is in the best interest of the child).		Ind. Code Ann. § 31-17-2-15.

STATE	COURT MAY AWARD JOINT CUSTODY	PRESUMPTION OF JOINT CUSTODY	STATUTORY GUIDELINES PROVIDED
Iowa	Iowa Code Ann. § 598.41(2) (court shall consider granting joint custody...if the court does not grant joint custody the court shall cite clear and convincing evidence that joint custody is not in the child's best interest).		Iowa Code Ann. § 598. 41(3).
Kansas	Kan. Stat. Ann. § 60-1610(a) (4)(A) (court may award joint custody).		Kan. Stat. Ann. § 60-1610(a)(3)(B).
Kentucky	Ky. Rev. Stat. Ann. § 403. 270(5) (court may award joint custody if it is in the best interest of the child). *Awn v. Awn*, 911 S.W.2d 612 (Ky. App. 1995) (joint custody does not require an equal division of physical custody).		Ky. Rev. Stat. Ann. § 403. 270(2).
Louisiana		La. Rev. Stat. Ann. § 9:335 (court shall order joint custody except for good cause shown).	La. Civ. Code Ann. art. 134.
Maine		Me. Rev. Stat. Ann. tit. 19- A. § 1653(2)(A) (joint custody presumed where both parties agree)	Me. Rev. Stat. Ann. tit. 19-A. § 1653(3).
Maryland	Md. Code Ann. Fam. Law § 5-203(d)(1) (court may award joint custody).		No statute
Massachusetts	Mass. Gen. Laws Ann. ch. 208 §31 (court may award shared custody).		No statute
Michigan	Mich. Stat. Ann. § 722.26a(1) (court may award joint custody). Mich. Stat. Ann. § 722.26a(1) (court shall consider awarding joint custody at the request of either parent and shall state on the record the reasons for granting or denying the request).		Mich. Stat. Ann. § 722. 26a(3).
Minnesota		Minn. Stat. Ann. *518.17(Subd. 2) (presumption of joint custody upon request of either or both parents).	Minn. Stat. Ann. *518.17 (Subd. 1).
Mississippi		Miss. Code Ann. § 93-5- 24(4) (presumption of joint custody where both parties agree).	Miss. Code Ann. § 93-5-24.
Missouri	Mo. Rev. Stat. § 452.375(5) (court may consider joint custody).		Mo. Rev. Stat. § 452.375(2).

Table D1: *State-by-State Summary of the Applicable Laws for Custody Determinations* (continued)

STATE	COURT MAY AWARD JOINT CUSTODY	PRESUMPTION OF JOINT CUSTODY	STATUTORY GUIDELINES PROVIDED
Montana	Mont. Rev. Code Ann. § 40-4-234 (the allocation of parenting functions may be included in the parenting plan).		Mont. Rev. Code Ann. § 40-4-212(1).
Nebraska	Neb. Rev. Stat. Ann. § 42-364(5) (court may award joint custody where both parties agree and it is in the best interests of the child).		Neb. Rev. Stat. Ann. § 42-364(2).
Nevada	Nev. Rev. Stat. Ann. § 125.490(2) (court may award joint legal custody without awarding joint physical custody).	Nev. Rev. Stat. Ann. § 125.490(1) (presumption of joint custody if both parents agree).	Nev. Rev. Stat. Ann. § 125.480(4).
New Hampshire		N.H. Rev. Stat. Ann. § 461-A:5 (presumption of joint decision making responsibility).	N.H. Rev. Stat. Ann. § 461-A:6.
New Jersey	N.J. Stat. Ann. § 9:2-4 (court may award joint custody if it is in the best interest of the child).		N.J. Stat. Ann. § 9:2-4.
New Mexico		N.M. Stat. Ann. § 40-4-9.1 (presumption of joint custody).	N.M. Stat. Ann. § 40-4-9.1.
New York	No specific statute concerning joint custody. N.Y. Dom. Rel. Law § 240 (court shall award custody in the best interest of the child). *Braiman v. Braiman,* 44 N.Y.2d 584 (1978) (joint custody may or may not include an arrangement for alternating physical custody).		No statute
North Carolina	N.C. Gen. Stat. § 50-13.2 (court may award joint custody).		No statute
North Dakota	No specific statute concerning joint custody. N.D. Cent. Code § 14-0906.2 (court shall award custody in the best interest of the child). *Lapp v. Lapp,* 293 N.W.2d 121 (N.D. 1980) (joint custody may be awarded if it is in the best interest of the child).		N.D. Cent. Code § 14-09-06.2.
Ohio	Ohio Rev. Code Ann. 3109.04(A) (court may award a shared parenting order if it is in the best interest of the child).		Ohio Rev. Code Ann. 3109.04(F)(1).
Oklahoma	Okl. Stat. tit. 43, § 109 (court may award joint custody upon the request of either parent).		Okl. Stat. tit. 43, § 109.

STATE	COURT MAY AWARD JOINT CUSTODY	PRESUMPTION OF JOINT CUSTODY	STATUTORY GUIDELINES PROVIDED
Oregon	Or. Rev. Stat. § 107.105 (court may award joint custody).		Or. Rev. Stat. § 107.137.
Pennsylvania	23 Penn. Cons. Stat. § 5304 (court may award joint custody if it is in the best interest of the child).		23 Penn. Cons. Stat. § 5303.
Rhode Island	No statute concerning joint custody. Cok v. Cok, 479 A.2d 1184 (R.I. 1984) (award of joint custody was within the discretion of the trial court)		No statute
South Carolina	No statute concerning joint custody. Scott v. Scott, 579 S.E.2d 620 (S.C. 2003) (exception circumstances existed to warrant joint custody).		No statute
South Dakota	S.D. Codified Laws § 25-5-7.1 (court may award joint custody).		No statute
Tennessee	Tenn. Code Ann. § 36-6-101(a)(2)(A) (court may award joint custody if it is in the best interest of the child).	Tenn. Code Ann. § 36-6-101(a)(2)(A) (presumption of joint custody where both parents agree).	Tenn. Code Ann. § 36-6-106.
Texas	Tex. Fam. Code Ann. § 153.134(a) (court may award joint custody if it is in the best interest of the child).		No statute
Utah	Utah Code Ann. § 30-3-10.2 (court may award joint custody if it is in the best interest of the child).		Utah Code Ann. § 30-3-10.2.
Vermont	Vt. Stat. Ann. tit. 15, § 665 (court may order shared parental rights and responsibilities when it is in the best interest of the child).		Vt. Stat. Ann. tit. 15, § 665(b).
Virginia	Va. Code Ann. § 20-124.2(B) (court may award joint custody if it is in the best interest of the child).		Va. Code Ann. § 20-124.3.
Washington	Wash. Rev. Code Ann. § 26.09.184 (court may allocate decision-making authority to one or both parents).		Wash. Rev. Code Ann. § 26.09.187(3).
West Virginia	W. Va. Code Ann. § 48-9-207 (court may award joint decision-making responsibility if it is in the best interest of the child).	W. Va. Code Ann. § 48-9-207 (presumption of joint decision-making responsibility if parents have been exercising a reasonable share of parenting functions for the child).	W. Va. Code Ann. § 48-9-206, -208.
Wisconsin		Wis. Stat. Ann. § 767.24(2) (presumption of joint legal custody).	Wis. Stat. Ann. § 767.24(5).

Appendix E:

Noncustodial Parent Access to Records

A concern for social workers is whether or not a noncustodial parent may access social workers' therapy records concerning their children. Most states allow either parent equal access to records unless there is language in the court order or custody decree that provides otherwise. For example, Alaska Statute § 25.20.130 states, "A parent who is not granted custody...has the same access to the medical, dental, school, and other records of the child as the custodial parent." State statutes generally allow court discretion to limit a noncustodial parent's access to records. For example, Pennsylvania Constitutional Statute § 5309 states, "The court, in its discretion, may determine not to release any part or parts of the information in this section but in doing so must state its reasons for denial on the record."

States vary concerning exactly which records noncustodial parents may access. Furthermore, some states allow treating professionals to withhold one parent's address if there are concerns about danger to that parent. Many states have broadly worded statutes allowing access by noncustodial parents to virtually all records pertaining to their children. For example, Montana Code § 40-4-225 states, "access to records and information pertaining to a minor child, *including but not limited* to medical, dental, law enforcement, and school records, may not be denied to a parent who is a party to a parenting plan."

However, some states have narrowly worded statutes that limit noncustodial parents to only the types of records listed in the statute. Maryland Code, Family Law § 9-104 states, "Unless otherwise ordered by a court, access to *medical, dental,* and *educational* records concerning the child may not be denied to a parent because the parent does not have physical custody of the child."

Some states allow a treating professional to withhold one parent's address if there are concerns about danger to the child or the custodial parent. Massachusetts General Laws ch. 208 § 31 states, "If nondisclosure of the present or prior address of the child or a party is necessary to ensure the safety or welfare of such child or party, the court may order that any part of such record pertaining to such address shall not be disclosed to such noncustodial parent."

Finally, if the courts have formally terminated a parent's rights, then that parent has no recognizable legal rights under any parental laws. This situation is generally limited to instances of severe abuse or neglect and/or where an adoption has occurred. This is distinct from the more common scenario in which a parent may have limited visitation rights, but retains full *legal* rights, including the rights to access medical records and to make decisions regarding the child's wellbeing.

The following chart provides a state-by-state summary of the applicable laws for noncustodial parents' access to records. Column 2 lists the relevant statutory citation governing access to records and Column 3 provides excerpts of text from the access to records laws.

This table was prepared as of February 2006. Interested parties should refer to the specific statutes or regulations or contact their state social work board for current statutes and regulations.

Table E1: *State-by-State Summary of the Applicable Laws for Noncustodial Parents' Access to Records*

STATE	RELEVANT STATUTE	RELEVANT TEXT
Alabama	Ala. Code § 30-3-154	§ 30-3-154. Availability of records to both parents. Unless otherwise prohibited by court order or statute, all records and information pertaining to the child, including, but not limited to, medical, physiological, dental, scholastic, athletic, extracurricular, and law enforcement, shall be equally available to both parents, in all types of custody arrangements.
Alaska	Alaska Stat. § 25.20.130	Sec. 25.20.130 Access to records of the child. A parent who is not granted custody under AS 25.20.060 - 25.20.130 has the same access to the medical, dental, school, and other records of the child as the custodial parent.
Arizona	Ariz. Rev. Stat. Ann. § 25-403(H)	§ 25-403. Custody; drug offenses; best interests of child; joint custody; domestic violence; modification of decree; fees... H. Unless otherwise provided by court order or law, on reasonable request both parents are entitled to have equal access to documents and other information concerning the child's education and physical, mental, moral and emotional health including medical, school, police, court and other records directly from the custodian of the records or from the other parent. A person who does not comply with a reasonable request shall reimburse the requesting parent for court costs and attorney fees incurred by that parent to force compliance with this subsection. A parent who attempts to restrict the release of documents or information by the custodian under this subsection without a prior court order is subject to appropriate legal sanctions.
Arkansas	Ark. Code Ann. § 9-13-301	§ 9-13-301. Non-custodial parent with visitation rights; right to scholastic records of child... .(b) Any noncustodial parent who has been awarded visitation rights by the court with respect to a child shall, upon request, be provided a copy of the current scholastic records of such child by the school district or college attended by the child.
California	Cal. Fam. Code § 3025	§ 3025. Parental access to records. Notwithstanding any other provision of law, access to records and information pertaining to a minor child, including, but not limited to, medical, dental, and school records, shall not be denied to a parent because that parent is not the child's custodial parent.
Colorado	Colo. Rev. Stat. Ann. § 14-10-123.8	§ 14-10-123.8. Access to records. Access to information pertaining to a minor child, including but not limited to medical, dental, and school records, shall not be denied to any party allocated parental responsibilities, unless otherwise ordered by the court for good cause shown.

STATE	RELEVANT STATUTE	RELEVANT TEXT
Connecticut	Conn. Gen. Stat. Ann. § 46b-56(e)	§ 46b-56. Superior Court orders re custody, care, therapy, counseling and drug and alcohol screening of minor children or parents in actions for dissolution of marriage, legal separation and annulment. Access to records of minor children by noncustodial parent. Parenting education program. (e) A parent not granted custody of a minor child shall not be denied the right of access to the academic, medical, hospital or other health records of such minor child unless otherwise ordered by the court for good cause shown.
Delaware	Del. Code Ann. tit. 13, § 727(a)	§ 727 Custody. (a) Whether the parents have joint legal custody or 1 parent has sole legal custody of a child, each parent has the right to receive, on request, from the other parent, whenever practicable in advance, all material information concerning the child's progress in school, medical treatment, significant developments in the child's life, and school activities and conferences, special religious events and other activities in which parents may wish to participate and each parent and child has a right to reasonable access to the other by telephone or mail. The Court shall not restrict the rights of a child or a parent under this subsection unless it finds, after a hearing, that the exercise of such rights would endanger a child's physical health or significantly impair his or her emotional development.
District of Columbia	D.C. Code Ann. § 16-914(a) (1)(B)(i)	§ 16-914. Custody of children. (B) For the purposes of this paragraph, the term: (i) "Legal custody" means legal responsibility for a child. The term "legal custody" includes the right to make decisions regarding that child's health, education, and general welfare, the right to access the child's educational, medical, psychological, dental, or other records, and the right to speak with and obtain information regarding the child from school officials, health care providers, counselors, or other persons interacting with the child…
	D.C. Code Ann. § 16-914(a)(3)(C)(8)	§ 16-914. Custody of children. (C) In any custody proceeding under this chapter, the Court may order each parent to submit a detailed parenting plan which shall delineate each parent's position with respect to the scheduling and allocation of rights and responsibilities that will best serve the interest of the minor child or children. The parenting plan may include, but shall not be limited to, provisions for…(8) access to the child's educational, medical, psychiatric, and dental treatment records…
Florida	Fla. Stat. Ann. § 61.13(2)(b)(3)	61.13. Custody and support of children; visitation rights; power of court in making orders…3. Access to records and information pertaining to a minor child, including, but not limited to, medical, dental, and school records, may not be denied to a parent because the parent is not the child's primary residential parent. Full rights under this subparagraph apply to either parent unless a court order specifically revokes these rights, including any restrictions on these rights as provided in a domestic violence injunction. A parent having rights under this subparagraph has the same rights upon request as to form, substance, and manner of access as are available to the other parent of a child, including, without limitation, the right to in-person communication with medical, dental, and education providers.

STATE	RELEVANT STATUTE	RELEVANT TEXT
Idaho	Idaho Code § 32-717A	32-717A Parents' access to records and information. Notwithstanding any other provisions of law, access to records and information pertaining to a minor child including, but not limited to, medical, dental, health, and school or educational records, shall not be denied to a parent because the parent is not the child's custodial parent. However, information concerning the minor child's address shall he deleted from such records to a parent, if the custodial parent has advised the records custodian in writing to do so.
Illinois	750 Ill. Comp. Stat. Ann. 5/602.1(e)	5/602.1. Parental powers; joint custody; criteria. (e) Notwithstanding any other provision of law, access to records and information pertaining to a child, including but not limited to medical, dental, child care and school records, shall not be denied to a parent for the reason that such parent is not the child's custodial parent; however, no parent shall have access to the school records of a child if the parent is prohibited by an order of protection from inspecting or obtaining such records pursuant to the Illinois Domestic Violence Act of 1986, as now or hereafter amended.
Iowa	Iowa Code Ann. § 598. 41(e)	598.41. Custody of children...1. e. Unless otherwise ordered by the court in the custody decree, both parents shall have legal access to information concerning the child, including but not limited to medical, educational and law enforcement records.
Kansas	Kan. Stat. Ann. § 16-60-1 610(4)(B)	60-1610. Decree; authorized orders. A decree in an action under this article may include orders on the following matters:...(4) Types of legal custodial arrangements. Subject to the provisions of this article, the court may make any order relating to custodial arrangements which is in the best interests of the child. The order shall provide one of the following legal custody arrangements, in the order of preference:...(B) Sole legal custody. The court may order the sole legal custody of a child with one of the parties when the court finds that it is not in the best interests of the child that both of the parties have equal rights to make decisions pertaining to the child. If the court does not order joint legal custody, the court shall include on the record specific findings of fact upon which the order for sole legal custody is based. The award of sole legal custody to one parent shall not deprive the other parent of access to information regarding the child unless the court shall so order, stating the reasons for that determination...
Louisiana	La. Rev. Stat. Ann. § 9:351	§ 351. Access to records of child. Notwithstanding any provision of law to the contrary, access to records and information pertaining to a minor child, including but not limited to medical, dental, and school records, shall not be denied to a parent solely because he is not the child's custodial or domiciliary parent.

STATE	RELEVANT STATUTE	RELEVANT TEXT
Maine	Me. Rev. Stat. Ann. tit. 19-A, § 1653(2)(D)(4)	§ 1653. Parental rights and responsibilities...2. Parental rights and responsibilities; order. This subsection governs parental rights and responsibilities and court orders for parental rights and responsibilities...D. The order of the court awarding parental rights and responsibilities must include the following:...(4) A statement that each parent must have access to records and information pertaining to a minor child, including, but not limited to, medical, dental and school records and other information on school activities, whether or not the child resides with the parent, unless that access is found not to he in the best interest of the child or that access is found to be sought for the purpose of causing detriment to the other parent. If that access is not ordered, the court shall state in the order its reasons for denying that access:
Maryland	Md. Code Ann., Fam. Law § 9-104	§ 9-104. Availability of records; noncustodial parent. Unless otherwise ordered by a court, access to medical, dental, and educational records concerning the child may not be denied to a parent because the parent does not have physical custody of the child.
Massachusetts	Mass. Gen. Laws Ann. ch. 208 § 31	§ 31. Custody of children; shared custody plans... The entry of an order or judgment relative to the custody of minor children shall not negate or impede the ability of the non-custodial parent to have access to the academic, medical, hospital or other health records of the child, as he would have had if the custody order or judgment had not been entered; provided, however, that if a court has issued an order to vacate against the non-custodial parent or an order prohibiting the noncustodial parent from imposing any restraint upon the personal liberty of the other parent or if nondisclosure of the present or prior address of the child or a party is necessary to ensure the health, safety or welfare of such child or party, the court may order that any part of such record pertaining to such address shall not be disclosed to such non-custodial parent.
Michigan	Mich. Stat. Ann. § 722.30	722.30. Noncustodial parents' access to records or information. Sec. 10. Notwithstanding any other provision of law, a parent shall not be denied access to records or information concerning his or her child because the parent is not the child's custodial parent, unless the parent is prohibited from having access to the records or information by a protective order. As used in this section, "records or information" includes, but is not limited to, medical, dental, and school records, day care provider's records, and notification of meetings regarding the child's education.
Minnesota	Minn. Stat. Ann. § 518.17(Subd. 3)	518.17. Custody and support of children on judgment...Subd. 3. Custody order(b) The court shall grant the following rights to each of the parties, unless specific findings are made under section 518.68, subdivision 1. Each party has the right of access to, and to receive copies of, school, medical, dental, religious training, and other important records and information about the minor children. Each party has the right of access to information regarding health or dental insurance available to the minor children...

STATE	RELEVANT STATUTE	RELEVANT TEXT
Mississippi	Miss. Code Ann. § 93-5- 24(5)	§ 93-5-24. Custody order; access to information; custody by parent with history of perpetrating family violence…An award of joint physical and legal custody obligates the parties to exchange information concerning the health, education and welfare of the minor child, and unless allocated, apportioned or decreed, the parents or parties shall confer with one another in the exercise of decision-making rights, responsibilities and authority.
Missouri	Mo. Rev. Stat. § 452.375(10)	452.375. Custody of children—standard—relevant factors—public policy—parental exchange of information—preferences—joint custody—access to records—domestic violence… 10. Unless a parent has been denied custody rights pursuant to this section or visitation rights under section 452.400, both parents shall have access to records and information pertaining to a minor child, including, but not limited to, medical, dental, and school records. If the parent without custody has been granted restricted or supervised visitation because the court has found that the parent with custody or any child has been the victim of domestic violence, as defined in section 455.200, RSMo, by the parent without custody, the court may order that the reports and records made available pursuant to this subsection not include the address of the parent with custody or the child. Unless a parent has been denied custody rights pursuant to this section or visitation rights under section 452.400, any judgment of dissolution or other applicablecourt order shall specifically allow both parents access to such records and reports.
Montana	Mont. Rev. Code Ann. § 40-4-225	40-4-225. Access to records by parent. Notwithstanding any other provision of law, access to records and information pertaining to a minor child, including but not limited to medical, dental, law enforcement, and school records, may not be denied to a parent who is a party to a parenting plan.
Nebraska	Neb. Rev. Stat. Ann. § 42-364(4)	§ 42-364. Dissolution or legal separation; decree; parenting plan; children; custody determination; rights of parents; child support; termination of parental rights; court; duties; modification proceedings…(4) Regardless of the custody determination of the court, (a) each parent shall continue to have full and equal access to the education and medical records of his or her child unless the court orders to the contrary and (b) either parent may make emergency decisions affecting the health or safety of his or her child while the child is in the physical custody of such parent pursuant to a visitation order entered by the court.
Nevada	Nev. Rev. Stat. Ann. § 125. 520(2)	125.520. Plan for carrying out court's order; access to child's records…2. Access to records and other information pertaining to a minor child, for example, medical, dental and school records, must not be denied to a parent for the reason that the parent is not the child's custodial parent.

STATE	RELEVANT STATUTE	RELEVANT TEXT
New Jersey	N.J. Stat. Ann. § 40-9:2-4.2	9:2-4.2. Parental access to emancipated child's records. (a) Every parent, to the extent permitted by federal and state laws concerning privacy, except as prohibited by the federal and state law, shall have access to records and information pertaining to his or her unemancipated child, including, but not limited to, medical, dental, insurance, child care, and educational records, whether or not the child resides with the parent, unless that access is found by the court to be not in the best interest of the child or the access is found by the court to be sought for the purpose of causing detriment to the other parent. (b) The place of residence of either parent shall not appear on any records or information released pursuant to the provisions of this section. (c) A child's parent, guardian, or legal custodian may petition the court to have the parent's access to the record is not in the best interest of the child or that the access sought is for the purpose of causing detriment to the other parent, the court may order that access to the records be limited.
New Mexico	N.M. Stat. Ann. § 40-4.9.1(H)	§ 40-4.9.1. Joint custody; standard for determination; parenting plan....(H). Notwithstanding any other provisions of law, access to records and information pertaining to a minor child, including medical, dental, and school records, shall not be denied to a parent because that parent is not the child's physical custodial parent or because that parent is not a joint custodial parent.
Ohio	Ohio Rev. Code Ann. § 3109. 051(H)(1)	3109.051. Parenting time rights....(H) (1) Subject to section 3125.16 and division (F) of section 3319.321 of the Revised Code, a parent of a child who is not the residential parent of the child is entitled to access, under the same terms and conditions under which access is provided to the residential parent, to any record that is related to the child and to which the residential parent of the child legally is provided access, unless the court determines that it would not be in the best interest of the child for the parent who is not the residential parent to have access to the records under those same terms and conditions. If the court determines that the parent of a child who is not the residential parent should not have access to records related to the child under the same terms and conditions under which the parent who is not the residential parent is to have access to those records, shall enter its written findings of facts and opinion in the journal, and shall issue an order containing the terms and conditions to both the residential parent and the parent of the child who is not the residential parent. The court shall include in every order issued pursuant to this division notice than any keeper of a record who knowingly fails to comply with the order or division (H) of this section is in contempt of court. (2) Subject to section 3125.16 and division (F) of section 3319.321 of the Revised Code, subsequent to the issuance of an order under division (H)(1) of this section, the keeper of any record that is related to a particular child
Pennsylvania	Penn. Cons. Stat. § 20-7-100	§ 5309. Access to records and information. (a) General rule.—Except as provided in subsections (b) and (c), each parent shall be provided access to all the medical, dental, religious or school records of the child, the residence address of the child and of the other parent and any other information that the court deems necessary. (b) Court determination not to release information. The court, in its discretion, may determine not to release any part or parts of the information in this section but in doing so must state its reason for denial on the record.

STATE	RELEVANT STATUTE	RELEVANT TEXT
South Carolina	S.C. Code Ann. § 20-7-100	§ 20-7-100. Rights and duties of parents in regard to their minor children...Each parent, whether the custodial or noncustodial parent of the child. has equal access and the same right to obtain all educational records and medical records of their minor children and the right to participate in their children's school activities unless prohibited by order of the court. Neither parent shall forcibly take a child from the guardianship of the parent legally entitled to custody of the child.
South Dakota	S.D. Codified Laws § 25-5-7.3	25-5-7.3. Denial of access to certain records and information pertaining to minor child prohibited. Notwithstanding any other provision of law, access to records and information pertaining to a minor child, including, but not limited to, medical, including counseling, dental, including orthodontia, optometric and similar health care, and school records, may not be denied to a parent because such parent is not the child's primary residential parent.
Tennessee	Tenn. Code Ann. § 36-6-110(a)(4),(5)	Rights. (a) Except when the juvenile court or other appropriate court finds it not to be in the best interests of the affected child, upon petition by a non-custodial, biological parent for whom parental rights have not been terminated, the court shall grant the following parental rights: ... (4) The right to receive directly from the child's school, (upon written request which includes a current mailing address and upon payment of reasonable costs of duplication), copies of the child's report cards, attendance records, names of teachers, class schedules, standardized test scores and any other records customarily made available to parents; (5) The right to receive copies of the child's medical records directly from the child's doctor or other health care provider, (upon written request which contains a current mailing address and upon payment of reasonable costs of duplication); ... (b) Any of the foregoing rights may be denied in whole or in part by the court upon a showing that such denial is in the best interests of the child.
Texas	Tex. Fam. Code Ann. §153.073	§ 153.073. Rights of Parent at All Times. (a) Unless limited by court order, a parent appointed as a conservator of a child has at all times the right:...(3) of access to medical, dental, psychological, and educational records of the child...
Vermont	Vt. Stat. Ann. tit. 15, § 670	§ 670 Access to records. Access to records and information pertaining to a minor child, including but not limited to medical, dental. law enforcement and school records shall not be denied to a parent solely because that parent has not been awarded parental rights and responsibilities. The court may order that access to all or a portion of the records or information shall be denied if access is not in the best interest of the child or if access may cause detriment to the other parent including but not limited to abuse.

STATE	RELEVANT STATUTE	RELEVANT TEXT
Virginia	Va. Code Ann. § 20-124.6	§ 20-124.6. Access to minor's records. A. Notwithstanding any other provision of law, neither parent, regardless of whether such parent has custody, shall be denied access to the academic or health records of that parent's minor child unless otherwise ordered by the court for good cause shown or pursuant to subsection B. In the case of health records, access may also he denied if the minor's treating physician or the minor's treating clinical psychologist has made a part of the minor's record a written statement that, in the exercise of his professional judgment, the furnishing to or review by the requesting parent of such health records would be reasonably likely to cause substantial harm to the minor or another person. If a health care entity denies a parental request for access to, or copies of, a minor's health record, the health care entity denying the request shall comply with the provisions of subsection F of § 32.1-127.1:03. The minor or his parent, either or both, shall have the right to have the denial reviewed as specified in subsection F of § 32.1-127.1:03 to determine whether to make the minor's health record available to the requesting parent. C. For the purposes of this section, the meaning of the term "health record" or the plural thereof and the term "health care entity" shall be as defined in subsection B of § 32.1-127.1:03.
	Va. Code Ann. § 32.1-127.1:03	§ 32.1-127.1:03. Health records privacy... As used in this section: "Health care entity" means any health care provider, health plan or health care clearinghouse. "Health care provider" means those entities listed in the definition of "health care provider" in § 8.01-581.1, except that state-operated facilities shall also be considered health care providers for the purposes of this section. Health care provider shall also include all persons who are licensed, certified, registered or permitted or who hold a multistate licensure privilege issued by any of the health regulatory boards within the Department of Health Professions, except persons regulated by the Board of Funeral Directors and Embalmers or the Board of Veterinary Medicine..."Health record" means any written, printed or electronically recorded material maintained by a health care entity in the course of providing health services to an individual concerning the individual and the services provided. "Health record" also includes the substance of any communication made by an individual to a health care entity in confidence during or in connection with the provision of health services or information otherwise acquired by the health care entity about an individual in confidence and in connection with the provision of health services to the individual.
	Va. Code Ann. § 8.01-581.1	§ 8.01-581.1. Definitions. As used in this chapter... "Health care provider" means (i) a person, corporation, facility or institution licensed by this Commonwealth to provide health care or professional services as a...clinical social worker...

Table E1: *State-by-State Summary of the Applicable Laws for Noncustodial Parents' Access to Records* (continued)

STATE	RELEVANT STATUTE	RELEVANT TEXT
Washington	Wash. Rev. Code Ann. § 26.09.225	26.09.225. Access to child's education and health care records. (1) Each parent shall have full and equal access to the education and health care records of the child absent a court order to the contrary. Neither parent may veto the access requested by the other parent. (2) Educational records are limited to academic, attendance, and disciplinary records of public and private schools in all grades kindergarten through twelve and any form of alternative school for all periods for which child support is paid or the child is the dependent in fact of the parent requesting access to the records. (3) Educational records of postsecondary educational institutions are limited to enrollment and academic records necessary to determine, establish, or continue support ordered pursuant to RCW 26.19.090.
West Virginia	W. Va. Code Ann. § 18-9-601	§ 48-9-601. Access to a child's records. (a) Each parent has full and equal access to a child's educational records absent a court order to the contrary. Neither parent may veto the access requested by the other parent. Educational records are academic, attendance and disciplinary records of public and private schools in all grades kindergarten through twelve and any form of alternative school. Educational records are any and all school records concerning the child that would otherwise be properly released to the primary custodial parent... (b) Each parent has full and equal access to a child's medical records absent a court order to the contrary. Neither parent may veto the access requested by the other parent. If necessary, either parent is required to authorize medical providers to release to the other parent copies of any and all information concerning medical care provided to the child which would otherwise be properly released to either parent... (c) Each parent has full and equal access to a child's juvenile court records, process and pleadings, absent a court order to the contrary. Neither parent may veto any access requested by the other parent. Juvenile court records are limited to those records which are normally available to a parent of a child who is a subject of the juvenile justice system.
Wisconsin	Wis. Stat. Ann. § 767.24(2)	767.24. Custody and physical placement. (4) Allocation of physical placement... (7) Access to records. (a) Except under par. (b) or unless otherwise ordered by the court, access to a child's medical, dental and school records is available to a parent regardless of whether the parent has legal custody of the child. A parent who has been denied periods of physical placement with a child under this section is subject to s. 118.125(2)(m) with respect to that child's school records, s. 51.30(5)(bm) with respect to the child's court or treatment records, s. 55.07 with respect to the child's records relating to protective services and s. 146.835 with respect to the child's patient health care records.
Wyoming	Wyo. Stat. Ann. § 20-2-201(e)	§ 20-2-201 Disposition and maintenance of children in decree or order; access to records... Unless otherwise ordered by the court, the noncustodial parent shall have the same right of access as the parent awarded custody to any records relating to the child of the parties, including school records, activities, teachers and teachers' conferences as well as medical and dental treatment providers and mental health records.

Endnotes

[1] Robert L. Barker, *The Social Work Dictionary* (Linda Beebe ed., 3rd ed., 1995) (stating that 'minor' is "[t]he legal designation for a child or adolescent, used to distinguish the different rights, protections, and privileges that exist for adults and for these youths").

[2] *See* Alaska Stat. §25.20.010, 25.20.020; Ariz. Rev. Stat. Ann. §1-215; Ark. Code Ann. §9-25-101; Cal. Fam. Code §6501; Colo. Rev. Stat. Ann. §2-4-401; Conn. Gen. Stat. Ann. §13-22-101; Conn. Gen. Stat. Ann. §1-1d; Del. Code Ann. tit. 1, §701; D.C. Code Ann. §46-101; Fla. Stat. Ann. §743.01, 743.07; Ga. Code Ann. §39-1-1; Haw. Rev. Stat. Ann. §577-1; Idaho Code §32-101; 750 111. Comp. Stat. Ann. 30/3-1; Ind. Code Ann. §1-1-4-5; Iowa Code Ann. §599.1; Kan. Stat. Ann. §38-101; Ky. Rev. Stat. Ann. §2.015; La. Civ. Code Ann. art. 29; Me. Rev. Stat. Ann. tit. 1, §73; Md. Ann. Code art. 1, §24; Mass. Gen. Laws Ann. ch. 231, §85P; Mich. Comp. Laws Ann. §722.52; Minn. Stat. Ann. §645.451(Subd. 5); Miss. Code Ann. §1-3-27, 41-4-51; Mo. Ann. Stat. §431005, 431061; Mont. Code Ann. §41-1-102; Neb. Rev. Stat. Ann. §43-210L Nev. Rev. Stat. Ann. §129.010; N.H. Rev. Stat. Ann. §21-B:1; N.J. Stat. Ann. §9:17B-3; N.M. Stat. Ann. §28-6-1; N.Y. Dom. Rel. Law §2; N.C. Gen. Stat. §48A-2; N.D. Cent. Code §14-10-02; Ohio Rev. Code Ann. §3109.01; Okla. Stat. Ann. tit. 15, §13; Okla. Stat. Ann. tit. 63, §2601; Or. Rev. Stat. §109.510; 1 Penn. Cons. Stat. Ann. §1991; R.I. Gen. Laws §15-12-1; S.C. Const. Art. II, §4; S.D. Codified Laws §26-1-1; Tenn. Code Ann. §1-2-1 13; Texas Civ. Prac. & Rem. Code Ann. §129.001; Utah Code Ann. §15-2-1; Vt. Stat. Ann. tit. I, §173; Va. Code Ann. §1-204; Wash. Rev. Code Ann. §26.28.010; W. Va. Code Ann. §2-3-1; Wis. Stat. Ann. §48.02; Wyo. Stat. Ann. §14-1-101.

[3] Ala. Code §26-1-1; Neb. Rev. Stat. Ann. §43-2101.

[4] Ind. Code Ann. §7.1-1-3-25; Miss. Code Ann. §67-3-53; 1 Penn. Cons. Stat. Ann. §1991.

[5] *See, e.g.,* Alaska Stat. §25.20.020; Iowa Code Ann. §599.1; Fla. Stat. Ann. §743.07; Md. Ann. Code art. I, §24(a)(2)(ii); Utah Code Ann. §15-2-1.

[6] Wis. Stat. Ann. §990.01.

[7] *See* Troxel v. Granville, 530 U.S. 57 (2000) (plurality opinion) ("So long as a parent adequately cares for his or her children (i.e., is fit), there will normally be no reason for the State to inject itself into the private realm of the family to further question the ability of that parent to make the best decisions concerning the rearing of…children.").

[8] Sheryl Brissett-Chapman, *Child Abuse and Neglect: Direct Practice, in* Encyclopedia of Social Work 353, 354 (Richard L. Edwards et al. eds., 19th ed. 2005).

[9] Harry D. Krause et. al., *Family Law* 428 of Dependent Children, S. Doc. No. 721, at 192 (2d Sess. 1909).

[10] *Id.* at 425 n.3.

[11] *See, e.g.,* Conn. Gen. Stat. Ann. §46h-150 ("Any minor who has reached such minor's sixteenth birthday and is residing in this state…may petition the superior court for juvenile matters or the probate court for the district in which either the minor or the parents or guardian of such minor resides for a determination that the minor named in the petition be emancipated.").

[12] Kathleen M. Quinn & Barbara A. Weiner, *Legal Rights of Children, in* Legal Issues in Mental Health Care 309, 311 (Barbara A. Weiner & Robert M. Wettstein, 1993). *See, e.g.,* W. Va. Code Ann. §49-7-27 ("Upon a showing that such child can *provide for his physical and financial well-being and has the ability to make decisions for himself,* the court may for good cause shown declare the child emancipated.") (emphasis added).

[13] Krause, *supra* note 9, at 425 n.3.

[14] Quinn, *supra* note 12, at 311.

[15] Ark. Code Ann. §20-9-602(7); Nev. Rev. Stat. Ann. §129.030(2).

16 *In re* E.G., 549 N.E.2d 322 (Ill. 1989); *In re* Rena, 705 N.E.2d 1155 (Mass. 1999); *In re* Swan, 569 A.2d 1202 (Me. 1990); *In re* Green, 292 A.2d 387 (Pa. 1972); Cardwell v. Bechtol, 724 S.W.2d 739 (Tenn. 1987). For a discussion of these cases *See* Christine M. Hanisco, Note & Comment, *Acknowledging the Hypocrisy: Granting Minors the Right to Choose Their Medical Treatment*, 16 N.Y.L. Sch. J. Hum. Rts. 899 (2000).

17 *See* discussion *infra* notes 21-24 and accompanying text.

18 Parental rights are protected under the Fourteenth Amendment of the U.S. Constitution. *See* Pierce v. Society of Sisters, 268 U.S. 510 (1925); Meyer v. Nebraska, 262 U.S. 39 (1923).

19 *See* Kimberly M. Mutcherson, *Whose Body Is It Anyway? An Updated Model of Healthcare Decision-Making Rights for Adolescents*, 14 Cornell J.L. & Pub. Pol'y 251 (2005) (discussing the law of healthcare decision-making for minors and the exceptions to the general rule).

20 *See, e.g.,* Ark. Code Ann. §20-9-602 (stating that "any one...of the following persons is authorized and empowered to consent...to any surgical or medical treatment or procedure not prohibited by law...(6) Any emancipated minor, for himself...").

21 Carey v. Population Services International, 431 U.S. 678 (1977); Planned Parenthood v. Danforth, 428 U.S. 52 (1976).

22 Mutcherson, *supra* note 19, at 263.

23 Ohio v. Akron Center for Reproductive Health. 497 U.S. 502 (1990).

24 *See, e.g.,* Ariz. Rev. Stat. Ann. §36-2152(A) ("A person shall not knowingly perform an abortion on a pregnant unemancipated minor unless the attending physician has secured the written consent from one of the minor's parents ... unless a judge of the superior court authorizes the physician to perform the abortion."); *see also* Ala. Code §26-21-3(e); Alaska Stat. §18.16.010(a)(3); Ark. Code Ann. §20-16-801 (parental consent required); Ark. Code Ann. §20-16-804 (judicial bypass); Cal. Health & Safety Code §123450; Del. Code Ann. tit. 24, §1783(b), 1784; Ga. Code Ann. §15- 11-112(b); Ind. Code Ann. §16-34-2-4(b); Kan. Stat. Ann. §65-6705(a); Ky. Rev. Stat. Ann. §311.732(2)(c); La. Civ. Code Ann. art. 40:1299.35.5(A)(2); Me. Rev. Stat. Ann. tit. 22, §1597A(2)(D); Mass. Gen. Laws Ann. ch. 112, §12S; Mich. Comp. Laws Ann. §722.52(Sect. 3)(2); Miss. Code Ann. §41-41-53(3); Mo. Ann. Stat. §188.020(3); Mont. Code Ann. §50-20-212; Nev. Rev. Stat. Ann. §442.255(2); N.C. Gen. Stat. §90-21.7(h); N.D. Cent. Code §18 Penn. Cons. Stat. Ann. §3206(c); R.I. Gen. Laws §23-4.7-6; S.C. Code Ann. §44-41-32; S.D. Codified Laws §34-23A-7; Tenn. Code Ann. §37-10-303(b); Texas Fam. Code Ann. §33.003; W. Va. Code Ann. §16-2F-4(a); Wis. Stat. Ann. §48.375(4)(b); Wyo. Stat. Ann. §35-6-118(a).

25 Ala. Code §22-8-6; Alaska Stat. §25.20.025(a)(4); Ariz. Rev. Stat. Ann. §44-132.01; Ark. Code Ann. §20-16-508; Cal. Fam. Code §6926; Colo. Rev. Stat. Ann. §25-4-402; Conn. Gen. Stat. Ann. §39a-592; Del. Code Ann. §tit. 13, §710; D.C. Mun. Regs. tit. 22, §600.7; Fla. Stat. Ann. §384.30; Ga. Code Ann. §37-7-8; Haw. Rev. Stat. Ann. §577A2; Idaho Code §39-4302, -4303; 410 Ill. Comp. Stat. Ann. 210/4; Ind. Code Ann. §16-36-1-3; Iowa Code Ann. §139A.35; Kan. Stat. Ann. §65-2892; Ky. Rev. Stat. Ann. §214.185; La. Civ. Code Ann. art. 1095: Me. Rev. Stat. Ann. tit. 22, §1502, 1823; Md. Code Ann. art. 20, §102(6)(3); Mass. Gen. Laws Ann. ch. III, §117; Mich. Comp. Laws Ann. §333.5127; Minn. Stat. Ann. §l44.343(Subd. I); Miss. Code Ann. §41-41-13; Mo. Ann. Stat. §431.061(4)(b); Mont. Code Ann. §41-1-402(2)(c); Neb. Rev. Stat. §71-504; Nev. Rev. Stat. Ann. §129.060; N.H. Rev. Stat. Ann. §141-C:18.11; N.J. Stat. Ann. §9:17A-4; N.M. Stat. Ann. §24-1-9; N.Y. Pub. Health Law §2305; N.C. Gen. Stat. §90-21 .5(a)(i); N.D. Cent. Code §14-10-17; Ohio Rev. Code Ann. §3709.241; Okla. Stat. Ann. tit. 63, §2602(a)(2); Or. Rev. Stat. §109.610; 35 Penn. Cons. Stat. Ann. §10103; R.I. Gen. Laws §23-8-1.1; S.C. Code Ann. §20-7-280, -290; S.D. Codified Laws §34-23-16; Tenn. Code Ann. §68-10-104(3); Texas Fam. Code Ann. §32.003(a)(3); Utah Code Ann. §26-6-18; Vt. Stat. Ann. tit. 18, §4226(a)(2); Va. Code Ann. §54.1-2969(E)(1); Wash. Rev. Code Ann. §70.24.110; W. Va. Code Ann. §16-4-10; Wis. Stat. Ann. §252.11; Wyo. Stat. Ann. §35-4-131.

26 Ala. Code §22-8-6; Ariz. Rev. Stat. Ann. §36-2024, 44-133.01; Ark. Code Ann §20-9-602; Cal. Fam. Code §6929; Colo. Rev. Stat. Ann. §13-22-102; Conn. Gen. Stat. Ann. §17a-682; Del. Code Ann. tit. 16, 2210; D.C. Mun. Regs. tit. 22, §600,7; Fla. Stat. Ann. §349.499; Ga. Code Ann. §37-7-8; Haw. Rev. Stat. Ann. §577-26; Idaho Code §39-307; 410 Ill. Comp. Stat. Ann. 210/4; Iowa Code Ann. §125.33; Kan. Stat. Ann. §65-2892a; Ky. Rev. Stat. Ann. §214.185; La. Civ. Code Ann. art. 1095; Me. Rev. Stat. Ann. tit. 22, §1502, 1823; Md. Code

Ann. art. 20, §102(6)(1),(2); Mass. Gen. Laws Ann. ch. 112, §12E; Mich. Comp. Laws Ann. §333.6121; Minn. Stat. Ann. §144.343(Subd. 1); Miss. Code Ann. §41-41-14; Mo. Ann. Stat. §431.061(4)(c); Mont. Code Ann. §41-1-402(2)(c); Nev. Rev. Stat. Ann. §129.050; N.H. Rev. Stat. Ann. §318-B:12-a; N.J. Stat. Ann. §9:17A-4; N.Y. Ment. Hyg. Law §22.11; N.C. Gen. Stat. §90-21.5; N.D. Cent. Code §14-10-17; Ohio Rev. Code Ann. §3719.012; Okla. Stat. Ann. tit. 63, §2602(A)(3); Or. Rev. Stat. §109.675(1); 71 Penn. Cons. Stat. Ann. §1690.112 : R.I. Gen. Laws §14-5-3, -4 (parental consent required unless physician determines it to be deleterious to treatment); S.C. Code Ann. §20-7-280, -290; S.D. Codified Laws §34-20A-50; Tenn. Code Ann. §63-6-220; Tex. Fam. Code Ann. §32.003(a)(5); Vt. Stat. Ann. tit. 18, §4226; Va. Code Ann. §54.1-2969(E)(3); Wash. Rev. Code Ann. §70.96A.095; Wis. Stat. Ann. §51.47 (parental consent required in four situations).

[27] *See* Ala. Code §22-8-6; Ark. Code Ann. §20-9-602; Cal. Fam. Code §6924; Colo. Rev. Stat. Ann. §27-10-103; Conn. Gen. Stat. Ann. §17a-682; D.C. Mun. Regs. tit. 22, §600.7; Fla. Stat. Ann. §394.459; Ga. Code Ann. §37-320(a); Idaho Code §39-4502, -4503; 405 Ill. Comp. Stat. Ann. 5/3-501; Ky. Rev. Stat. Ann. §214.185; Md. Code Ann. art. 20, §102(d): Mich. Comp. Laws Ann. §330.1707(1); N.H. Rev. Stat. Ann. §135-C:12 (providing that a minor may consent independently to treatment at a state-run facility); N.M. Admin. Code §7.20.11.22(C)(3); N.C. Gen. Stat. §90-21.5(a)(iv); Ohio Rev. Code Ann. §5122.04; Or. Rev. Stat. §109.675: 35 Penn. Cons. Stat. Ann. §10101.1; Tex. Fam. Code Ann. §32.003, 32.004; Va. Code Ann. §54.1-2969(E)(4); Wash. Rev. Code Ann. §71.34.500.

[28] *See In re E.G.*, 549 N.E.2d 322 (Ill. 1989) (finding that a 17-year-old member of the Jehovah's Witnesses could refuse a blood transfusion); Cardwell v. Bechtol, 724 S.W.2d 739 (Tenn. 1987) (finding that a 17-year-old minor could consent to medical treatment by an osteopath); Belcher v. Charleston Area Medical Center, 422 S.E.2d 827 (W. Va. 1992) ("We agree with the holding of *Caldwell,* and we believe that the mature minor exception is part of the common law rule of parental consent of this state."). *But see* Powers v. Floyd, 904 S.W.2d 713 (Tex. Ct. App. 1995) ("Texas has never adopted or recognized the mature minor exception.").

[29] Mutcherson, *supra* note 19, at 268.

[30] Ark. Code Ann. §20-9-602 (stating that [a]ny unemancipated minor of sufficient intelligence to understand and appreciate the consequences of the proposed surgical or medical treatment or procedures" may consent to the treatment); Nev. Rev. Stat. Ann. §129.030(2)("[T]he consent of the parent or parents or the legal guardian of a minor is not necessary for a local or state health officer, board of health, licensed physician or public or private hospital to examine or provide treatment for any minor…who understands the nature and purpose of the proposed examination or treatment and its probable outcome, and voluntarily requests it.").

[31] Ala. Code §22-8-3; Ariz. Rev. Stat. Ann. §36-2271, 44-132; Del. Code Ann. tit. 13, §707(b)(5)(ii); Fla. Stat. Ann. §743.064; 410 Ill. Comp. Stat. Ann. 210/3; Kan. Stat. Ann. §65-2891; Minn. Stat. Ann. 144.344; Miss. Code Ann. §41-41-7; Mont. Code Ann. §41-1-402(d); Nev. Rev. Stat. Ann. §129.030(1)(d); N.Y. Pub. Health Law §2504; N.C. Gen. Stat. §90-21.5; N.D. Cent. Code §14-10-17.1; Okla. Stat. Ann. tit. 63, §2602(A)(7); S.D. Codified Laws §20-94.2; Tenn. Code Ann. §63-6-222.

[32] *See, e.g.,* Del. Code Ann. tit. 13, §707(b)(5)(ii) (stating that "consent shall be effective only after reasonable efforts shall have been made to obtain the consent of the parent or guardian of said minor"); Tenn. Code Ann. §63-6-222(b) (stating that "[s]uch treatment shall be commenced only after a reasonable effort is made to notify the minor's parents or guardian, if known or readily ascertainable").

[33] *See, e.g.,* Or. Rev. Stat. §109.675(2) (stating that "the person providing treatment shall have the parents of the minor involved before the end of treatment unless the parents refuse or unless there are clear clinical indications to the contrary, which shall be documented in the treatment record"); Vt. Stat. Ann. tit. 18, §4226(b) (stating that "[t]he parent, parents or legal guardian shall be notified by the physician if the condition of a minor child requires immediate hospitalization as the result of drug usage, alcoholism or for the treatment of a venereal disease").

[34] 45 C.F.R. §164.502(g)(3) (2003).

[35] 45 C.F.R. §164.502(g)(3)(i)(c) (2003).

[36] National Association of Social Workers, *Code of Ethics* §1.07(b) (revised 1999) ("Privacy and Confidentiality"), *available at* **http://www.socialworkers.org/pubs/code/code.asp** (last visited Aug. 3, 2006).

---

[37] National Association of Social Workers, *NASW Standards for the Practice of Social Work with Adolescents*, at http://www.socialworkers.org/practice/standards/sw_adolescents.asp (last visited Aug. 3, 2006).

[38] *Id.* at §1.07(c).

[39] Tarasoff v. Regents of University of California, 551 P.2d 334 (Cal. 1976).

[40] *Id.*

[41] For a discussion of social workers and the duty to warn see Sandra Kopels & Jill Doner Kagel, *Do Social Workers Have a Duty to Warn?*, 67 Soc. Serv. Rev. 101 (1993).

[42] *See* National Association of Social Workers Legal Defense Fund, *Social Workers and the Duty to Warn* (2005), *at* https://www.naswdc.org/ldf/legal_issue/200502.asp (last visited Aug. 3, 2006) (this article is available online to NASW members).

[43] A "next friend" is a person, usually a relative, who appears in court on behalf of a minor, but who is not a party to the lawsuit. For example, children are often represented in court by their parents as "next friends."

[44] A "guardian *ad litem*" is a person, who is often, but not always, a lawyer, appointed by the court to represent the best interests of a child in a court action that might affect them.

[45] *See, e.g.*, Alaska Stat. §25.24.310; Ark. Code Ann. §16-61-104; Fla. R. Civ. P. 1.210(h); Haw. Rev. Stat. Ann. §551-2; Kan. Stat. Ann. §60-217; Me. Rev. Stat. Ann. tit. 19-A, §1507; Mich. Court R. 2.201(b); Minn. R. Civ. P. 17.02; N.J. Stat. Ann. §2A:4A-39; Wis. Stat. Ann. §803.01(3).

[46] *See, e.g.*, Kan. Stat. Ann. §60-217 ("The court shall appoint a guardian *ad litem* for a minor or incapacitated person not otherwise represented in an action…"); Minn. R. Civ. P. 17.02 ("A party who is an infant or incompetent and is not represented shall be represented by a guardian *ad litem* appointed by the court in which the action is pending or is to be brought."); Wis. Stat. Ann. §803.01(3) ("A guardian *ad litem* shall be appointed in all cases where the minor or incompetent has no general guardian of property, or where the general guardian fails to appear and act on behalf of the ward or incompetent…").

[47] *See, e.g.*, Alaska Stat. §25.24.310 ("the court may, upon the motion of a party to the action or upon its own motion, appoint an attorney or the office of public advocacy to represent a minor with respect to the custody, support, and visitation of the minor or in any other legal proceeding involving the minor's welfare…"); Me. Rev. Stat. Ann. tit. 19-A, §1507 ("the court may appoint a guardian *ad litem* for the child…").

[48] Me. Rev. Stat. Ann. tit. 19-A, §1507.

[49] Me. Rev. Stat. Ann. tit. 22, §4005.

[50] Me. Rev. Stat. Ann. tit. 18-A, §1-403(4).

[51] *See, e.g.*, Ariz. Rev. Stat. Ann. §44-131 (stating that "[a] person who is married to an adult is not under legal disability because of that person's minority to make a contract and a contract made by that person is not invalid or voidable because of that person's minority"). *See also* Conn. Gen. Stat. §46h-150d; Fla. Stat. Ann. §743.01; Haw. Rev. Stat. Ann. §577-25; 750 Ill. Comp. Stat. Ann. 30/5; Nev. Rev. Stat. Ann. §129.130; N.M. Stat. Ann. §32A-21-5; N.C. Gen. Stat. §7B-3507; Or. Rev. Stat. §419B.552; Va. Code Ann. §16.1-334; W. Va. Code Ann. §49-7-27.

[52] *See, e.g.*, Ark. Code Ann. §4-59-101(c); D.C. Code Ann. §12-3505; Me. Rev. Stat. Ann. tit. 33, §52; Miss. Code Ann. §15-3-11; Mo. Ann. Stat §431.060; S.C. Code Ann. §20-7-250.

[53] *See, e.g.*, Mo. Ann. Stat. §442.080; Utah Code Ann. §15-2-2; Wash. Rev. Code Ann. §26.28.030.

[54] *See, e.g.*, Cal. Fam. Code §6924(e) (stating that "[t]he minor's parents or guardian are not liable for payment for mental health treatment or counseling services provided pursuant to this section unless the parent or guardian participates in the mental health treatment or counseling, and then only for services rendered with the participation of the parent or guardian").

[55] Brown v. Board of Education, 347 U.S. 483, 493 (1954) (noting that education, as the principal means of teaching children cultural values as well as vocational or career skills, is "perhaps the most important function of state and local government"). The Supreme Court, in *Brown*, held that segregation of children in public schools solely on the basis of race deprives the children of the minority

group of equal educational opportunities and is, therefore, a violation of the Equal Protection Clause of the Fourteenth Amendment. *Id.* Furthermore, in *Plyer v. Doe*, the Supreme Court held that a state could not deny public education to children who were not "legally admitted" into the United States. *Plyer v. Doe*, 457 U.S. 202, 230 (1982). The Court noted that public education is not "merely some 'governmental benefit' indistinguishable from other forms of social welfare legislation. Both the importance of education in maintaining our basic institutions, and the lasting impact of its deprivation on the life of the child, mark the distinction." *Id.* at 221.

[56] *See* Pierce v. Society of Sisters, 268 U.S. 510 (1925) (holding that a state statute that compelled attendance in a public school between the ages of eight and sixteen unreasonably interfered with the rights of parents to make child-rearing decisions, including the education of their children in church-operated schools). *See also* Wisconsin v. Yoder, 406 U.S. 205 (1972); Medeiros v. Kiyosaki, 478 P.2d 314 (Haw. 1970).

[57] *See* Ala. Code §16-28-1, -3, -5; Alaska Stat. §14.30.010(a); Ariz. Rev. Stat. Ann. §15-802(A)(1); Ark. Code Ann. §6-18-201; Cal. Educ. Code §482(X); Colo. Rev. Stat. Ann. §22-33-104; Conn. Gen. Stat. Ann. §10-184; Del. Code Ann. tit. 14, §2702; D.C. Code Ann. §31-202; Fla. Stat. Ann. §1003.21; Ga. Code Ann. §20-2-690.1; Haw. Rev. Stat. Ann. §302A-1132; Idaho Code §33-202; 105 Ill. Comp. Stat. Ann. 5/26-1; Ind. Code Ann. §20-33-2-6; Iowa Code Ann. §299.1; Kan. Stat. Ann. §72-1111; Ky. Rev. Stat. Ann. §159.010; La. Rev. Stat. Ann. §17:221; Me. Rev. Stat. Ann. tit. 20-A, §5001-A; Md. Code Ann., Educ. §7-301(a); Mass. Gen. Laws Ann. ch. 76, §1; Minn. Stat. Ann. §120A.22; Miss. Code Ann. §37-13-91; Mo. Ann. Stat. §167.031; Mont. Code Ann. §20-5-102; Neb. Rev. Stat. Ann. §79-201; Nev. Rev. Stat. Ann. §392.040; N.H. Rev. Stat. Ann. §193:1; N.J. Stat. Ann. §18A:38-25; N.M. Stat. Ann. §22-12-2; N.Y. Educ. Law §3204; N.C. Gen. Stat. §115C-378; N.D. Cent. Code §15.1-20-01; Ohio Rev. Code Ann. §3321.04; Okla. Stat. Ann. tit. 70, §10-015; Or. Rev. Stat. §339.010; Pa. Stat. Ann. tit. 24, §13-1327(a); R.I. Gen. Laws §16-19-1; S.C. Code Ann. §59-65-10; S.D. Codified Laws §13-27-1; Tenn. Code Ann. §49-6-3001(c); Tex. Educ. Code Ann. §21.085; Utah Code Ann. §53A-11-101; Vt. Stat. Ann. tit. 16, §1121; Va. Code Ann. §22.1-254; Wash. Rev. Code Ann. §28A.225.010; W. Va. Code Ann. §18-8-1; Wis. Stat. Ann. §118.15; Wyo. Stat. Ann. §21-4-102.

[58] The Supreme Court has not yet ruled on any aspect of home-schooling and, as a result, state case law is sparse and inconsistent. *See generally* Jack Macmullan, Comment, *The Constitutionality of State Home Schooling Statutes*, 39 Vill. L. Rev. 1309 (1994) (discussing the various state approaches to home schooling). The majority of states explicitly exempt home-schooling from compulsory school attendance laws if the home education plan meets specific statutory requirements. *See* Ala. Code §16-28-1, -3, -5; Alaska Stat. §14.30.010(a); Ariz. Rev. Stat. Ann. §15-802(A)(1); Ark. Code Ann. §6-18-201; Cal. Educ. Code §48200; Colo. Rev. Stat. Ann. §22-33-104; Conn. Gen. Stat. Ann. §10-184; Del. Code Ann. tit. 14, §2702; D.C. Code Ann. §31-202; Fla. Stat. Ann. §1003.21; Ga. Code Ann. §20-2-690.1; Haw. Rev. Stat. Ann. §302A-1132; Idaho Code §33-202; 105 Ill. Comp. Stat. Ann. 5/26-1; Ind. Code Ann. §20-33-2-6; Iowa Code Ann. §299.1; Kan. Stat. Ann. §72-1111; Ky. Rev. Stat. Ann. §159.010; La. Rev. Stat. Ann. §17:221; Me. Rev. Stat. Ann. tit. 20-A, §5001-A; Md. Code Ann., Educ. §7-301(a); Mass. Gen. Laws Ann. ch. 76, §1; Minn. Stat. Ann. §120A.22; Miss. Code Ann. §37-13-91; Mo. Ann. Stat. §167.031; Mont. Code Ann. §20-5-102; Neb. Rev. Stat. Ann. §79-201; Nev. Rev. Stat. Ann. §392.040; N.H. Rev. Stat. Ann. §193:1; N.J. Stat. Ann. §18A:38-25; N.M. Stat. Ann. §22-12-2; N.Y. Educ. Law §3204; N.C. Gen. Stat. §115C-378; N.D. Cent. Code §15.1-20-01; Ohio Rev. Code Ann. §3321.04; Okla. Stat. Ann. tit. 70, §10-015; Or. Rev. Stat. §339.010; Pa. Stat. Ann. tit. 24, §13-1327(a); R.I. Gen. Laws §16-19-1; S.C. Code Ann. §59-65-10; S.D. Codified Laws §13-27-1; Tenn. Code Ann. §49-6-3001(c); Tex. Educ. Code Ann. §21.085; Utah Code Ann. §53A-11-101; Vt. Stat. Ann. tit. 16, §1121; Va. Code Ann. §22.1254; Wash. Rev. Code Ann. §28A.225.010; W. Va. Code Ann. §18-8-1; Wis. Stat. Ann. §118.15; Wyo. Stat. Ann. §21-4-102. Thirteen states that have not passed legislation explicitly providing for home-schooling allow home-schooling that is "substantially equivalent" to the education a child would receive in the public school. *See* Alaska Stat. §14.30.010(b)(11); Conn. Gen. Stat. Ann. §10-184; Del. Code Ann. tit. 14, §2703; Idaho Code §33-202; Ind. Code Ann. §20-8.1-3-34; Ind. Code Ann. §20-33-2-8; Me. Rev. Stat. Ann. tit. 20-A, §5001-A(3); Md. Code Ann., Educ. §7-301(a); Mass. Gen. Laws Ann. ch. 76, §1; Nev. Rev. Stat. Ann. §392.070; N.J. Stat. Ann. §18A:38-25; Okla. Stat. Ann. tit. 70, §10-105; S.D. Codified Laws §13-27-3. Some states have determined that home-schools may qualify as private schools if they meet all of the statutory requirements of a private school. *See* Ala. Code §16-28-1, -3; Cal. Educ. Code §48222; 105 Ill. Comp. Stat. Ann. 5/26-1(1); Kan. Stat. Ann. §72-1111; Ky. Rev. Stat. Ann. §159.030(1)(b); Mich. Comp. Laws Ann. §380.1561(3)(a); Neb. Rev. Stat. Ann. §79-201(b); Tex. Educ. Code Ann. §21.086.

[59] Individuals with Disabilities Act, 20 U.S.C. § 1401(a)(8). For a discussion of "frequently asked questions" concerning the IDEA see Committee on Education and the Workforce, *Individuals with Disabilities Education Act (IDEA): Guide to Frequently Asked Questions.* at http://edworkforce.house.gov/issues/109th/education/idea/ideafaq.pdf (Feb. 17, 2005).

[60] A "free appropriate public education" is defined as "special education and related services." 20 U.S.C. § 1401(a)(8). "Related services" include transportation, and such developmental, corrective, and other supportive services (including speech pathology and audiology, psychological services, physical and occupational therapy, recreation, including therapeutic recreation, social work services, including rehabilitation counseling, and medical services, *except* that such medical services shall be for diagnostic and evaluation purposes only) as may be required to assist a child with a disability to benefit from special education, and includes the early identification and assessment of disabling conditions in children. *Id.* at (a)(22).

[61] *See generally* Jane Nusbaum Feller et al., *Working with the Courts in Child Protection,* U.S. Department of Health and Human Services: Administration for Children and Families, Administration on Children, Youth and Families National Center on Child Abuse and Neglect 52-57 (1992) (discussing the competency of children as witnesses). *See also* Ala. Code § 12-21-165 (children who do not understand the nature of an oath are incompetent to testify); Ariz. Rev. Stat. Ann. § 12-2202 (in a civil proceeding, children under age 10 who are incapable of receiving just impressions of the facts about which they are asked to testify are incompetent to testify); Colo. Rev. Stat. Ann. § 13-90-106 (children under age 10 who are incapable of receiving just impressions of the facts about which they are asked to testify are incompetent to testify); Fla. Stat. Ann. § 90.605 (child may testify without taking oath if child understands the duty to tell the truth); Ga. Code Ann. § 24-9-7 (court determines competency to testify); Kan. Stat. Ann. § 60-417 (person is disqualified as a witness if incapable of expressing himself or understanding the duty to tell the truth); La. Civ. Code Ann. art. 13:3665 (competent witness is a person of proper understanding); La. Civ. Code Ann. art. 115 (child witness need not be placed under oath if court can assure that child understands the duty to speak the truth): Minn. Stat. Ann. § 595.06 (court may examine child's capacity to understand the nature and obligation of an oath); N.Y. Crim. Proc. Law § 65.20 (child under age 9 may not testify under oath unless the child understands the nature of an oath); Ohio Rev. Code Ann. § 2317.01 (child under age 10 who is incapable of receiving just impressions of the facts and transactions of which he or she is examined is incompetent to testify); Tex. R. Evid. 601 (child who does not possess sufficient intelligence to relate transactions with respect to which he or she is interrogated is not competent to testify).

[62] *See, e.g.,* Mo. Ann. Stat. § 491.060 (providing that a child under age 10 is incompetent to testify, except that a child under age 10 who is an alleged victim of a crime against the person, sexual offense or crime against the family is a competent witness).

[63] *See* Ariz. Rev. Stat. Ann. § 13-4061 (every person is competent to testify in a criminal trial); Ark. R. Evid. 601; Cal. Evid. Code § 700, 701 (unless that person is incapable of expressing himself or understanding the duty to tell the truth); Del. R. Evid. 601: Fla. Stat. Ann. § 90.601-602; Ga. Code Ann. § 24-9-I: 725 Comp. Stat. Ann. 5/115-14 (unless that person is incapable of expressing himself or understanding the duty to tell the truth); Ind. Code Ann. § 34- 45-2-1, 35-37-4-1; Iowa R. Evid. 5.601; Md. R. Evid. 5-601: Mass. Gen. Laws Ann. ch. 233, § 20 (any person of sufficient understanding may testify); Mich. R. Evid. 600.1 (unless that person is incapable of expressing himself or understanding the duty to tell the truth); Minn. Stat. Ann. § 595.02 (providing that every person of sufficient understanding may testify); Mont. R. Evid. 601 (unless that person is incapable of expressing himself or understanding the duty to tell the truth); Nev. R. Evid. 601 (unless that person is incapable of expressing himself or understanding the duty to tell the truth); N.M. R. Evid. 11-601; N.Y. Crim. Proc. Law § 60.20 (every person of sufficient intelligence is competent to testify); N.C. Gen. Stat. § 601 (unless that person is incapable of expressing himself or understanding the duty to tell the truth); Ohio Rev. Code Ann. § 2317.01; Okla. Stat. Ann. tit. 17, § 2601; 42 Penn. Cons. Stat. Ann. § 5911; S.D. Codified Laws § 19-14-1; Tex. R. Evid. 601; Utah Code Ann. § 74-24-2; Vt. R. Evid. 601 (unless that person is incapable of expressing himself or understanding the duty to tell the truth); Wash. Rev. Code Ann. § 5.60.020 (every person of sound mind may testify); W. Va. R. Evid. 601; Wis. Stat. Ann. § 906.01.

[64] *See, e.g.,* Commissioner. v. Monzon, 744 N.E.2d 1131 (Mass. App. Ct. 2001) (court used a two-prong test of competency: the ability to observe and remember and the ability to understand the difference between truth and falsehood).

[65] See, e.g., Colo. Rev. Stat. Ann. §13-25-129 (hearsay statement of a child under age 15 who is an alleged victim of a sexual offense may be admissible); Ga. Code Ann. §24-3-16 (hearsay statement of a child under age 14 describing sexual contact or physical abuse may be admissible); Mont. Code Ann. §46-16-220 (hearsay statement of a child who is an alleged victim of a sexual offense or crime of violence may be admissible); Tex. Crim. Proc. Code Ann. §38.072 (hearsay statement of a child under age 12 who is an alleged victim of child abuse may he admissible); Utah Code Ann. §76-5-411 (hearsay statement of child under age 14 who is an alleged victim of sexual abuse may be admissible); Wash. Rev. Code Ann. §9A.44.120 (hearsay statement of a child under age 10 who is an alleged victim of a sex offense or physical abuse may he admissible).

[66] See, e.g., Ark. Code Ann. §16-44-203 (videotaped statement to child under age 17 who is an alleged victim of a sexual offense may be admissible): Colo. Rev. Stat. Ann. §18-3-413 (videotaped statement of a child under age 15 who is an alleged victim of a sexual offense may he admissible); Ind. Code Ann. §35-37-4-6 (videotaped statement of a child under age 14 may be admissible); Mich. Comp. Laws Ann. §600.2163a (videotaped statement of a child under age 16 may be permitted); Neb. Rev. Stat. Ann. §29-1926 (videotaped statement of a child under age 11 may be permitted); N.D. Cent. Code §34-04-04.1 (videotaped statement of a child who is an alleged victim of a sexual offense may be permitted).

[67] See, e.g., N.Y. Crim. Proc. Law §65.20.

[68] See, e.g., Mich. Comp. Laws Ann. §600.2163a.

[69] See, e.g., Neb. Rev. Stat. Ann. §29-1926 (in camera testimony of a child under age 11 may be permissible).

[70] See, e.g., Mich. Comp. Laws Ann. §600.2163a; Neb. Rev. Stat. Ann. §29-1926.

[71] Dr. John A. Gaudiosi et al., Child Maltreatment 2003, U.S. Department of Health and Human Services: Administration for Children and Families, Administration on Children, Youth and Families Children's Bureau xiii (2005), available at http://www.acf.hhs.gov/programs/cb/pubs/cm03/cm2003.pdf (last visited Aug. 3, 2006).

[72] Id.

[73] Id. at xvii.

[74] National Association of Social Workers, Child Abuse and Neglect, in Social Work Speaks: National Association of Social Workers Policy Statements 32, 34 (Paula L. Delo et al., eds., 6th ed. 2003).

[75] Id. at 35.

[76] For a discussion of mandatory reporting statutes and the ethical considerations that they raise see generally Carolyn 1. Polowy & Peter McLeod, Social Workers & Child Abuse Reporting: A Review of State Mandatory Reporting Requirements, Nat'l Assoc. Social Workers (2000) [hereinafter Child Abuse Reporting] (this law note may be purchased from NASW).

[77] Id.

[78] National Association of Social Workers, Code of Ethics §1.01 (revised 1999) ("Commitment to Clients"), available at http://www.socialworkers.org/pubs/code/code.asp (last visited Aug. 3, 2006).

[79] Child Abuse Reporting, supra note 76, at 17.

[80] National Association of Social Workers Legal Defense Fund, Is it Necessary for Protective Services Social Workers to Obtain a Warrant to Investigate a Child Abuse or Neglect Complaint?, at https://www.socialworkers.org/ldf/legal_issue/200306.asp (last visited Aug. 3, 2006) (this article is available online to NASW members).

[81] Id.

[82] For a discussion of the relevant cases see id.

[83] Id.

[84] 547 S.E.2d 451 (N.C. Ct. App. 2001).

[85] In North Carolina, the county Departments of Social Services received over 113,557 reports of suspected abuse or neglect in 2003. Of those reports, 27,310 were confirmed cases of child abuse. Furthermore, at least 30 deaths in North Carolina in 2003, were attributed to child abuse.

[86] *Id.* at 453.

[87] *Id.* at 455.

[88] 582 S.E.2d 255 (N.C. 2003)

[89] *Id.* at 288 ("Had there been a complaint of a parent of lack of supervision of the child or other credible evidence that indicated a serious failing on the part of the parents to look after the child, then such conduct could rise to the level of triggering the investigative mandate of N.C.G.S. §7B-302. However, a single report of a naked, unsupervised two-year-old in the driveway of her home does not trigger the investigative requirements of N.C.G.S. §7B-302.").

[90] *See* Roska v. Peterson, 328 F.3d 1230 (2003).

[91] *See* Snell v. Tunell, 920 F.2d 673, (10th Cir. 1990); Landstrom v. Illinois Dep't of Children & Family Servs., 892 F.2d 670, 674-78 (7th Cir. 1990); Doe v. Hennepin, 858 F.2d 1325, 1329-30 (8th Cir. 1988), *cert. denied*, 490 U.S. 1108 (1989); Hodorowski v. Ray, 844 F.2d 1210, 1217 (5th Cir. 1988); Robison, 821 F.2d 913, 921-22 (2nd Cir. 1987).

[92] *See* Sheila B. Kamerman, *Families Overview*, *in* Encyclopedia of Social Work 927, 927 (Richard L. Edwards et al. eds., 19th ed. 2005) (defining "nuclear family" as "a small conjugal unit with one or two parents, a few children, and only limited ties with any but immediate kin").

[93] Barker, *supra* note 1, at 258.

[94] *Id.* at 931. A growth in women's labor force participation and changes in family law concerning marriage, divorce, abortion, and child custody have resulted in dramatic changes in the structure and composition of the family in the United States. *Id.* at 928.

[95] Tavia Simmons & Grace O'Neill, U.S. Census Bureau, *Households and Families: 2000*, Census 2000 Brief 6-7, *at* **http://www.census.gov/prod/2001pubs/c2kbr01-8.pdf** (issued September 2001). The number of unmarried-partner households increased from 3.5 percent of all households in 1990 to 5.2 percent in 2000. *Id.* at 7. Female family households with children under 18 years have increased from 6.6 percent of all households in 1990 to 7.2 percent of all households in 2000. *Id.* Male family households with children under 18 make up 2.1 percent of all households. *Id.* at 4. Finally, multigenerational families make up 3.7 percent of all family households. Multigenerational families may include (1) a householder living with his/her children and grandchildren; (2) a householder, his/her children, and his/her parent(s)/parent(s)-in-law; or (3) a householder, his/her children, his/her parent(s)/parent(s)-in-law, and his/her randchildren. *Id.* at 7-8.

[96] *Id.* at 1. "Grandparent caregiver" is defined as "people who had primary responsibility for their co-resident grandchildren younger than 18."

[97] *Id.* 431 U.S. 494 (1977) (holding that an ordinance making it a crime for a homeowner to live with her son and grandson and a second grandson who was a cousin of the first grandson was unconstitutional and violated due process).

[98] *Id.* at 504. The Court further noted that the history of the United States supports a larger conception of the family. *Id.* at 505.

[99] *See* Roe v. Wade. 410 U.S. 113 (1973); Stanley v. Illinois, 405 U.S. 645 (1972); Wisconsin v. Yoder, 406 U.S. 205 (1972); Ginsberg v. New York, 390 U.S. 629 (1968); Griswold v. Connecticut, 381 U.S. 479 (1965); Pierce v. Society of Sisters, 268 U.S. 510 (1925); Meyer v. Nebraska, 262 U.S. 39 (1923)

[100] *Moore*, 431 U.S. at 497.

[101] U.S. Census Bureau, *Unmarried-Partner Households by Sex of Partners*, Census 2000 Summary File 1, *at* **http://www.factfinder.census.gov/servlet/DTTable?_bin=y&-geo_id=01000US84-ds_name=DEC_2000_SFI_U&-Jang=en&-state=dt&-mt_name=DEC_2000_SFI_U_PCTO1484-format=&-CONTEXT=dt** (last visited Aug. 3, 2006). According to the Census 2000, there are 301,026 male householders living with male partners and 293,365 female householders living with female partners. *Id.*

[102] *See* Hernandez v. Robles, 805 N.Y.S.2d 354 (N.Y. Sup. Ct. 2005) (holding that domestic relations law disallowing same-sex marriage does not violate the due process or equal protection provisions of the New York Constitution); Samuels v. New York State Dept. of Health, 2006 WL 346465 (N.Y.

Sup. Ct. 2006) (holding there was a rational basis for construing New York Domestic Relations law as applying only to opposite sex marriages, precluding the claim by same sex couples that their state constitutional equal protection right to be married was violated); Li v. State, 110 P.3d 91 (Or. 2005) (holding that under Oregon law, marriage in Oregon is limited to opposite-sex couples and that since the effective date of the Oregon marriage initiative, marriage has been limited under the Oregon Constitution to opposite-sex couples). *But see* Goodridge v. Department of Public Health, 798 N.E.2d 941 (Mass. 2003) (holding that a Massachusetts marriage licensing statute that limited the protections, benefits and obligations of civil marriage to individuals of opposite sexes lacked a rational basis and violated the Massachusetts constitutional equal protection principles).

[103] *See In re* Baby Z, 724 A.2d 1035 (Conn. 1999) (denying lesbian co-parent the opportunity to adopt her partner's biological child); *In re* Adoption of Luke, 640 N.W.2d 374 (Neb. 2002) (holding that the child was not eligible for adoption by biological mother's same-sex partner under the Nebraska adoption statutes); *In re* Jane Doe, 711 N.E.2d 234 (Ohio 1999) (denying lesbian second-parent the ability to adopt her partner's biological child).

[104] *See* Pulliam v. Smith, 501 S.E.2d 898 (N.C. 1998) (upholding trial court's decision to modify child custody order and award exclusive custody of the child to the child's biological mother as a result of the biological father's homosexual relationship); *In re* Bonfield, 780 N.E.2d 241 (Ohio 2002) (cohabiting same-sex partner of child's biological parent is not children's "parent" for purposes of entering into a shared parenting agreement); Bottoms v. Bottoms, 457 S.E.2d 102 (Va. 1995) (holding that a person's sexual orientation is an important factor in determining a parent's unfitness in a custody case and awarding custody to the child's maternal grandmother rather than the child's biological parent). *But see* Boswell v. Boswell, 721 A.2d 662 (Md. 1998) (holding that a restriction in the custody decree prohibiting children from any contact with the noncustodial parent's same-sex partner was an abuse of the trial court's discretion); E.O. v. L.M., 711 N.E.2d 886 (Mass. 1999) (granting visitation between the child and the biological parent's former same-sex partner as a "de facto" parent); T.B. v. L.R.M., 786 A.2d 913 (Pa. 2001) (holding that the biological parent's same-sex partner had standing to bring an action for custody of the child); Inscoe v. Inscoe, 700 N.E.2d 70 (Ohio Ct. App. 1997) (holding that evidence was insufficient to support the determination that a custodial parent's sexual orientation, who was living in an openly homosexual relationship, had adversely impacted the child such that custody should be awarded to the biological mother).

[105] *See* John Laird, *Lesbians: Parenting, in* Encyclopedia of Social Work 1604, 1606 (Richard L. Edwards et al. eds., 19th ed. 2005).

[106] *Id.* There are several cases currently pending review that challenge state laws restricting the ability of same-sex couples to marry. For example, a Maryland circuit court recently held that a Maryland law denying same-sex couples the right to marry violates the Maryland constitution. Deane v. Conaway, 2006 WL 148145 (Md. Cir. Ct. 2006). The court stated, "When tradition is the guise under which prejudice or animosity hides, it is not a legitimate state interest..." *Id.* at 19. The state's appeal of the circuit court's decision is currently pending. *See also* Citizens for Equal Protection v. Bruning, 290 F.Supp.2d 1004 (Neb. Dist. Ct. 2005) (holding that a Nebraska statute denying same-sex couples the right to marry was in violation of the Nebraska constitution); Lewis v. Harris, 2003 W.L. 23191114 (N.J. Super. Ct. Law Div. 2003) (denying the right of same-sex couples to marry under New Jersey law).

[107] National Association of Social Workers, *Code of Ethics* §1.05(c) (revised 1999) ("Cultural Competence and Social Diversity") (emphasis added), *available at* **http://www.socialworkers.org/pubs/code/code.asp** (last visited Aug. 3, 2006).

[108] National Association of Social Workers, *Lesbian, Gay, and Bisexual Issues, in* Social Work Speaks: National Association of Social Workers Policy Statements 224, 224 (Paula L. Delo et al. eds., 6th ed., 2003).

[109] Kamerman, *supra* note 92, at 929.

[110] *Id.*

[111] *Infra* "Best Interests of the Child." Standard 24 et seq.

[112] Ardis L. Campbell, Annotation, *Determination of Status as Legal or Natural Parents in Contested Surrogacy Births,* 77 A.L.R.5th 567 (2005).

---

[113] Surrogacy is "[a] form of reproductive technology in which a man donates his sperm or a woman donates her egg or use of her body so that a fetus can be conceived and developed through to birth... Usually the surrogate mother who carries the fetus to delivery is paid and is contracted to relinquish the baby soon after birth." Barker, *supra* note 1, at 373.

[114] Krause, *supra* note 9, at 364-65.

[115] Jerald V. Hale, *From Baby M. to Jaycee B: Fathers, Mothers, and Children in the Brave New World*, 24 J. Contemp. L. 335, 335 (1998).

[116] *Id.* at 336.

[117] *Id.* at 342. The most common statutory provision simply declares all surrogacy contracts void and unenforceable. *See, e.g.*, N.Y. Dom. Rel. Law §122 (providing that "surrogate parenting contracts are hereby declared contrary to the public policy of this state, and are void and unenforceable"). Other states prohibit only those surrogacy contracts entered into for pecuniary gain. *See, e.g.*, Nev. Rev. Stat. Ann. §127.287. A few states have enacted legislation providing for the legality and enforceability of surrogacy arrangements; however, all allow the birth mother to rescind the surrogacy contract within a specified period after conception. *See, e.g.*, Va. Code Ann. §20-156 et seq.

[118] *See generally* Stephanie F. Schultz, *Surrogacy Arrangements: Who Are the "Parents" of a Child Born Through Artificial Reproductive Techniques?*, 22 Ohio N.U. L. Rev. 273 (1995).

[119] Malina Coleman, *Gestation, Intent, and the Seed: Defining Motherhood in the Era of Assisted Human Reproduction*, 17 Cardozo L. Rev. 497, 505 (1996).

[120] *See* Johnson v. Calvert, 851 P.2d 776, 782 (Cal. 1993) (stating that the genetic donors are "a couple who desired to have a child of their own genetic stock but are physically unable to do so without the help of reproductive technology. They affirmatively intended the birth of the child, and took steps necessary to effect *in vitro* fertilization. But for their acted-on intention, the child would not exist").

[121] *See* Belsito v. Clark, 67 Ohio Misc. 2d 54 (Ohio Misc. 1994) (holding that under Ohio law the natural parents of a child conceived through *in vitro* fertilization utilizing a gestational surrogate are the individuals who provided the genetic material for the child). *See also In re* Marriage of Moscheta, 25 Cal. App. 4th 1218 (Cal. Ct. App. 1994).

[122] Schultz, *supra* note 122, at 285-86.

[123] *Id.* at 287.

[124] The American Bar Association, Section of Family Law and the ABA Center for Continuing Legal Education, *Assisted Reproduction and Alternative Families* 2 (2005).

[125] *Id.*

[126] *See* discussion *infra* notes 110-13, 135-39 and accompanying text. For cases denying a same-sex co-parent the right to adopt the child *See infra* note 106.

[127] *See* discussion *infra* notes 237-43 and accompanying text. For cases concerning the ability of a same-sex, non-biological parent to be awarded custody and/or visitation with the child see *infra* note 107.

[128] *See* discussion *infra* notes 260-71 and accompanying text.

[129] Joyce E. Everett, *Child Foster Care, in* Encyclopedia of Social Work 375, 375 (Richard L. Edwards et al. eds., 19th ed. 2005).

[130] National Association of Social Workers, *Foster Care and Adoption, in* Social Work Speaks: National Association of Social Workers Policy Statements 144, 148 (Paula L. Delo et al. eds., 6th ed., 2003).

[131] Everett, *supra* note 155, at 376.

[132] *Id.* at 377.

[133] *Id.* at 377-78.

[134] *See* Social Security Act of 1935, Pub. L. No. 96-272, Tit. [V-E, ch. 531, 49 Stat. 620 (1936); Social Security Act of 1935, Pub. L. No. 96-270, Tit. IV-B, ch. 531, 49 Stat. 620 (1936); Social Security Act of 1935, Pub. L. No. 97-35, Tit. XX, ch. 531, 49 Stat. 620 (1936); Adoption Assistance and Child Welfare Act of 1980, Pub. L. No. 96-272, 94 Stat. 500 (1981).

[135] Adoption and Safe Family Act of 1997, Pub. L. No. 105-89, III Stat. 2115 (1998) (codified in scattered sections of 42 U.S.C. 1305 (1998).

[136] Libby S. Adler, *The Meanings of Permanence: A Critical Analysis of the Adoption and Safe Families Act of 1997*, 38 nary. J. on Legis. I, 8 (2001).

[137] *Id.* at 9.

[138] Adoption Assistance and Child Welfare Act of 1980, Pub. L. No. 96-272, 94 Stat. 5(X) (1981).

[139] *See generally* Adler, *supra* note 162 (analyzing family preservation and the termination of parental rights as policy considerations in foster care placement).

[140] Jacqueline D. Stanley, *Grounds for Termination of Parental Rights*, 32 Am. Jur. Proof of Facts 3d 83, §1 (2005).

[141] *Id.* at §3.

[142] *Id.*

[143] Stagnation occurs when there is a lack of change in parental capacity or circumstances after a substantial period of time. *Id.*

[144] Abandonment "evinces a settled purpose to forego all duties and relinquish all parental claims to a child. It involves more than a parent's nonsatisfaction of his or her legal obligations to the child...As a general rule, the abandonment must he willful." *Id.* at §4.

[145] Before a court can use mental incapacity as the basis for terminating parental rights, the court must establish that the mental disability "renders the parent unable to provide for the needs and well-being of his or her children." *Id.* at §5.

[146] Neglect itself may be found if a parent fails to provide support, suffers from alcoholism or drug abuse, fails to provide appropriate supervision, fails to provide a stable living environment and food, fails to maintain contact with a child, fails to correct problems within a reasonable amount of time, fails to protect a child from an abusive parent, fails to provide a clean home and child care, or fails to provide personal contact with the child. *Id.* at §6.

[147] *Id.* at §7.

[148] *Id.* at §7.1.

[149] *Id.* at §7.2.

[150] *Id.* at §7.3. *See, e.g., In re* C.M.S., 462 S.E.2d 398 (Ga. Ct. App. 1995).

[151] *Id.* at §7.4. *See, e.g., In re* O.R., 767 N.E.2d 872 (III. 2003).

[152] *Id.* at §2.

[153] *Id.*

[154] *Id. See also* Michael G. Walsh, *Standing of Foster Parent to Seek Termination of Rights of Foster Child's Natural Parents*, 21 A.L.R.4th 535 (discussing state and federal cases in which the courts have considered whether a foster parent, defined as any person not related to the biological parents who has been granted physical custody of the child, has standing to *Seek* termination of the parental rights of the natural parents). *See, e.g,* Ariz. Rev. Stat. Ann. §8-533 (allowing any person with a legitimate interest in the child to petition to terminate parental rights).

[155] Stanley, *supra* note 166, at §2. See *Walsh, supra* note 180, at §5 for a discussion of the cases where foster parents were not held to have standing to petition for the termination of the parental rights.

[156] *See* Richard L. Brown, *Disinheriting the "Legal Orphan": Inheritance Rights of Children After Termination of Parental Rights*, 70 Mo. L. Rev. 125, 132-33 n. 44-8 (2005) (citing Ariz. Rev. Stat. Ann. §8-539; Colo. Rev. Stat. §193-608(1); Conn. Gen. Stat. Ann. §45a-707(8); D.C. Code Ann. §16-2361(a); Haw. Rev. Stat. Ann. §571-63; Kan. Stat. Ann. §38-1583(f); Ky. Rev. Stat. Ann. §625.104; Me. Rev. Stat. Ann. tit. 22, §4056(1); Mont. Code Ann. §41-3-611(1); N.H. Rev. Stat. Ann. §170-C:12; N.C. Gen. Stat. §7B-1 112; Okla. Stat. Ann. tit. 10, §7006-1.3(A); S.C. Code Ann. §20-7-1576(A); Tenn. Code Ann. §36-1-113(1)(1); Utah Code Ann. §78-3a-413(1); Va. Code Ann. §64.15.1(5); Wyo. Stat. Ann. §14-2-317(a).

[157] *See, e.g.,* New Jersey v. TLO, 469 U.S. 325 (1985) (holding that the standard for searches of students in a public school is not probable cause, but the lower standard of reasonable suspicion).

[158] *See, e.g.,* Kingsley v. Kingsley. 623 So.2d 780 (Fla. Dist. Ct. App. 1993) (reversing trial court determination that eleven-year-old child had standing to initiate legal proceeding to terminate parental rights). In *Kingsley,* Gregory Kingsley, after his guardian *ad litem* failed to bring an action on his behalf, petitioned the Florida Circuit Court to terminate his biological parents' rights so his foster parents could adopt him. *Id.* at 782.

[159] *See, e.g.,* Twigg v. Mays, No. 88-4489-CA-01, slip op. at 6-7 (Ha. Cir. Ct. Aug. 18, 1993) (holding that the Florida Constitution allowed a minor legal standing to initiate proceeding). *See also* Virginia Mixon Swindell, *Children's Participation in Custodial and Parental Right Determinations,* 31 Hous. L. Rev. 659, 687-88 (1994); Jay C. Lauhscher, Note, A *Minor of 'Sufficient Age and Understanding' Should Have the Right to Petition for the Termination of the Parental Relationship,* 40 N.Y.L. Sch. L. Rev. 565 (1996).

[160] Swindell, *supra* note 185, at 680.

[161] Lauhscher, *supra* note 185, at 592 n.243; *see also,* Cal. Welf. & Inst. Code §317(c) (stating that if a child is the alleged victim of abuse, "the court shall appoint counsel for the child to advocate for the protection, safety, and…well being of the child" in all judicial proceedings); 705 Ill. Comp. Stat. Ann. 405/1-5 (stating that a child has "the right to be represented by counsel"); Mass. Gen. Laws Ann. ch. 119, §29 (stating that a child before the court "shall have…the right to counsel at all hearings"); N.Y. Fam. Ct. Act §249 (stating that "minors who are the subject of family court proceedings or appeals in proceedings originating in family court should be represented by counsel of their own choosing"); 42 Pa. Cons. Stat. Ann. §6337 (stating that a child is "entitled to representation by legal counsel at all stages of any proceedings").

[162] *See, e.g.,* Dept. of Human Resources v. Ammons, 426 S.E.2d 901, 903 (Ga. Ct. App. 1992) (rejecting a challenge to the outcome of a termination proceeding, finding that an appointment of an attorney or guardian *ad litem* for the child involved is not required in every termination proceeding); *In re* Kapcsos, 360 A.2d 174. 178 (Pa. 1976) (holding that a child has no constitutional right to counsel in a termination proceeding).

[163] *See, e.g.,* Nev. 1st Jud. Dist. Ct. R. 23 (leaving it to the discretion of the court to appoint counsel for a minor child).

[164] *See, e.g.,* Ariz. Rev. Stat. Ann. §8-519(C) ("All records and information in the possession of the foster care review hoard regarding children and their parents or relatives shall be deemed confidential."); Va. Code Ann. §63.2-104 (stating that the records of children in foster care are confidential and information about children in foster care or their parents or relatives is confidential).

[165] 22 Va. Admin. Code §40-910-100(B)(4).

[166] Virginia Department of Social Services, Vol. VII, sec. III, ch. B, §13.1, *Confidentiality of Records, available at* http://www.dss.virginia.gov/files/division/dfs/fc/fc_policy_manual/public_manual.pdf

[167] *See, e.g.,* Alaska Admin. Code tit. 7, §54.070; 22 Va. Admin. Code §40-910-100(B)(4) ("[C]lient records may be released to the guardian *ad litem* and the court appointed special advocate who are appointed for a child as a result of a court order or to attorneys representing the child or the child's parents.")

[168] *See, e.g.,* Alaska Admin. Code tit. 7, §54.030.

[169] Richard P. Barth, *Adoption, in* Encyclopedia of Social Work 48, 48 (Richard L. Edwards et al. eds., 19th ed. 2005).

[170] *Id.* at 49-50.

[171] Richard A. Leiter, *50 State Surveys, Family, Adoption,* National Survey of State Laws (2005).

[172] *Id.*

[173] Rose M. Kreider, U.S. Census Bureau, *Adopted Children and Stepchildren: 2000,* Census 2000 Special Reports (August 2003).

[174] *See, e.g.,* Ala. Code §26-10A-5(2) ("No rule or regulation of the Department of Human Resources or any agency shall prevent an adoption by a single person solely because such person is single or shall prevent an adoption solely because such person is of a certain age.").

[175] *See* Cal. Fam. Code §8802; Conn. Gen. Stat. Ann. §45a-724, 45a-731; D.C. Code Ann. §16-302; *In re* M.M.D., 662 A.2d 837 (D.C. 1995); *In re* Petition of K.M., 653 N.E.2d 888 (Ill. 1995); Mass. Gen. Laws Ann. ch. 210, §1; Adoption of Tammy, 619 N.E.2d 315 (Mass. 1993); Adoption of Galen, 680 N.E.2d 70 (Mass. 1997); N.J. Stat. Ann. §9:3-43; N.J. Admin. Code tit. 10, §121 C-4.1; *In re* Adoption of Two Children by H.N.R., 666 A.2d 553 (N.J. 1995); N.M. Stat. Ann. §32A-5-11; N.Y. Dom. Rel. Law §110; 18 NYCRR 421.16(h)(2); *In re* Adoption of Emilio R., 293 A.D.2d 27 (N.Y. App. Div. 2002); Vt. Stat. Ann. tit. 15A, §1-102; Vt. Stat. Ann. tit. 15, §1204; Adoptions of B.L.V.B. and E.L.V.B., 628 A.2d 1271 (Vt. 1993); Wis. Stat Ann. §48.82; Wis. Admin. Code §51.07.

[176] National Association of Social Workers, *Code of Ethics* §1.05(c) (revised 1999) ("Cultural Competence and Social Diversity"), *available at* http://www.socialworkers.org/pubs/code/code.asp (last visited Aug. 3, 2006).

[177] National Association of Social Workers, *Foster Care and Adoption, in* Social Work Speaks: National Association of Social Workers Policy Statements 144, 148 (Paula L. Delo et al. eds., 6th ed. 2003).

[178] *See* Defense of Marriage Act, H.R. 3396, 104th Cong. §1738C (1996). For a discussion of state case law concerning the adoption of children by same-sex partners *See* generally Sonja Larsen, *Adoption of Child by Same-Sex Partners*, 27 A.L.R.5th 54 (2005).

[179] *See, e.g.,* Fla. Stat. Ann. §63.042(3) (stating that "[n]o person eligible to adopt under this statute may adopt if that person is a homosexual"); Miss. Code Ann. §93-17-3(2) (stating that "Adoption by couples of the same gender is prohibited"); Utah Code Ann. §78-30-I(3)(b) (stating that [a] child may not he adopted by a person who is cohabiting in a relationship that is not a legally valid and binding marriage under the laws of this state. For purposes of this Subsection (3)(b), 'co-habiting' means residing with another person and being involved in a sexual relationship with that person").

[180] *News and Notes,* Adoptive Families, June 2006, at 10. Currently, only Florida, Mississippi, and Utah have legislation restricting the ability of gays and lesbians to adopt. Mississippi and Utah both deny adoption to same-sex couples. Miss. Code Ann. §93-17-3(2); Utah Code Ann. §78-30-1(3)(b). Florida is the only state that restricts the adoption and foster care of children to heterosexual individuals. Fla. Stat. Ann. §63.042(3) ("No person eligible to adopt under this statute may adopt if that person is a homosexual.").

[181] National Center for Lesbian Rights, *Second Parent Adoptions: A Snapshot of Current Law available at* http://www.nclrights.org/publications/2ndparentadoptions.htm (last visited Mar. 30, 2007).

[182] For a discussion of the benefits second-parent adoption for children *See* the following brief to which NASW signed in agreement: Brief of Amici Curiae Ohio Psychological Association, et al., *In re* Adoption of Jane Doe, 86 Ohio St. 3d 1408 (Ohio 1999) (No. 99-0215) (stating that the best interests of the child are served by the "social, financial, psychological and other types of security afforded the child by legal recognition of a child-parent relationship");. *See also* Joan Biskupic, *Same-sex couples redefining family law in USA,* USA Today, Feb. 17, 2003, *available at* http://www.usatoday.com/news/nation/2003-02-17-cover-samesex_x.htm (updated Feb. 18, 2003).

[183] *See* Sharon S. v. Superior Court, 73 P.3d 554 (Cal. 2003) (allowing a former domestic partner to complete a second-parent adoption of a biological child of the other partner during the partnership); *In re* Hart, 806 A.2d 1179 (Del. Fam. Ct. 2001) (holding that same-sex partner of adoptive parent had standing to bring petition to adopt partner's children where adoption would he in the best interests of the children); *In re* M.M.D., 662 A.2d 837 (D.C. 1995) (stating that same-sex couple living together in committed relationship may adopt a child and the fact that one of the parents has already adopted the child does not alter the second parent's adoption of the child); *In re* K.M, 653 N.E.2d 888 (Ill. 1995) (holding that same-sex partner of adoptive parent may join in adoption and original adoptive parent's relationship to child is unaltered by second-parent adoption); Mariga v. Flint, 822 N.E.2d 620 (Ind. Ct. App. 2005) (holding that court under the stepparent adoption statute may allow biological mother's domestic partner to adopt children); Adoption of Tammy, 619 N.E.2d 315 (Mass. 1993) (holding that same-sex partners may adopt a child); *In re* Adoption of a Child by J.M.G., 632 A.2d 550 (N.J. Super. Ct. Ch. Div. 1993) (holding that a second-parent adoption by the same-sex partner of child's biological parent would he in the best interests of the child); *In re* Evan, 583 N.Y.S.2d 997 (N.Y. 1992) (holding that lesbian partner of biological parent may adopt a child if the adoption is in the best interests of the child); *In re* Adoption of R.B.F., 803 A.2d 1195 (Pa. 2002) (holding that it was within the court's discretion to grant adoption of a child to same-sex partner of biological parent without termination of the legal parent's rights); Adoption of B.L.V.B. 628 A.2d 1271 (Vt. 1993) (holding that both the biological parent and her same-sex partner could adopt the biological parent's children together).

[184] *Supra,* note 181.

[185] *See, e.g.,* Matter of Adoption of T.K.J., 931 P.2d 488 (Colo.App.,1996) (denying lesbian couple the ability to adopt each other's natural child); *In re* Adoption of Luke, 640 N.W.2d 374 (Neb. 2002) (holding that the child was not eligible for adoption by biological mother's same-sex partner under the Nebraska adoption statutes); *In re* Jane Doe, 711 N.E.2d 234 (Ohio 1999) (denying lesbian second-parent the ability to adopt her partner's biological child); *In Interest of* Angel Lace M., 516 N.W.2d 678 (Wis. 1994) (denying mother's female co-habiting partner the ability to adopt her child under Wisconsin law).

[186] National Association of Social Workers, *Lesbian. Gay, and Bisexual Issues, in* Social Work Speaks: National Association of Social Workers Policy Statements 224, 228 (Paula L. Delo et al. eds., 6ᵗʰ ed. 2003).

[187] 73 P.3d 554 (Cal. 2003).

[188] Amicus Curiae Brief of National Association of Social Workers, Sharon S. v. Superior Court, 73 P.3d 554 (Cal. 2003).

[189] *Id.* at 4-5.

[190] *"Social Workers as Expert Witnesses"* August 2004, General Counsel Law Note.

[191] *See generally* Debra T. Landis, Annotation, *Admissibility of Social Worker's Testimony on Child Custody Issues,* 1 A.L.R.4ᵗʰ 837 (2005) (discussing state court cases expressing the ability of social workers to testify as to child custody).

[192] Those states include California, Colorado, Georgia, Indiana, Iowa, Louisiana, Maryland, Massachusetts, Minnesota, Montana, New York, North Carolina, South Dakota, Texas, Washington, Wisconsin. *See* Ohmer v. Superior Court, 196 Cal. Rptr. 224 (Cal. Ct. App. 1983); *In re* A.D., 706 P.2d 7 (Colo. Ct. App. 1985); Baker v. Smiley, 202 S.E.2d 39 (Ga. 1973); *In re* Adoption of Lockmondy, 343 N.E.2d 793 (Ind. Ct. App. 1976); *In re* C.W., 342 N.W.2d 885 (Iowa Ct. App. 1983); Ramos v. Ramos, 697 So.2d 280 (La. Ct. App. 1997); Montgomery County Dept. of Social Services v. Sanders, 381 A.2d 1154 (Md. Ct. Spec. App. 1977); Petition of Dept. of Public Welfare to Dispense with Consent to Adoption, 429 N.E.2d 1023 (Mass. App. Ct. 1982); Hoffa v. Hoffa, 382 N.W.2d 522 (Minn. Ct. App. 1986); *In re* C.L.A., 685 P.2d 931 (Mont. 1984); *In re* Dulay, 265 N.Y.S.2d 247 (N.Y. App. Div. 1965); Beck v. Beck, 207 S.E.2d 378 (N.C. Ct. App. 1974); *In re* E., 325 N.W.2d 840 (S.D. 1982); Garner v. Garner, 673 S.W.2d 413 (Tex. App. 1984); Dependency of Luntsford, 604 P.2d 195 (Wash. Ct. App. 1979); Fritschler v. Fritschler, 208 N.W.2d 336 (Wis. 1973).

[193] *See, e.g.,* Montgomery County Dept. of Social Services v. Sanders, 381 A.2d 1154 (Md. Ct. Spec. App. 1977).

[194] *See, e.g., In re* Marriage of Milovich, 434 N.E.2d 811 (Ill. App. Ct. 1982) (holding that since trial court was not hound by social worker's opinion as to which parent should have custody, it was not an abuse of discretion to disallow the testimony of the social worker).

[195] National Association of Social Workers, *Code of Ethics* §1.01 (revised 1999) ("Commitment to Clients"), *available at* http://www.socialworkers.org/pubs/code/code.asp (last visited Aug. 3, 2006).

[196] *See* Fed. R. Evid. 702.

[197] *See, e.g.,* Utah Ct. R. 4-903, *available at* http://www.utcourts.gov/resources/rules/ucja/ch04/4-903.htm (last visited Aug. 3, 2006).

[198] Cal. Fam. Code §31 10.5(c)(4).

[199] 2005 Cal. R. Ct. §5.225(d), (e).

[200] *Id.*

[201] National Association of Social Workers, *Code of Ethics* §1.04 (revised 1999) ("Competence"), *available at* http://www.socialworkers.org/pubs/code/code.asp (last visited Aug. 3, 2006).

[202] National Association of Social Workers, Oregon Chapter (2005). *Model Standards of Practice for Child Custody Evaluation, available at* http://www.nasworegon.org/resources/child custody/index.html_(last visited October 11, 2006).

203 *Guidelines for Child Custody Evaluations in Divorce Proceedings*, 49 American Psychologist No. 7, 677-680 (1994), *available at* http://www.apa.org/practice/childcustody.html (last visited Aug. 3, 2006).

204 American Academy of Child and Adolescent Psychiatry, *Summary of the Practice Parameters for Child Custody Evaluation, at* http://www.aacap.org/page.ww?section,Summaries&name.Summary +of+the+Practice+Parameters+for+Child+Custod y+Evaluation (last visited Aug. 3, 2006).

205 *See* Carolyn I. Polowy & Joel Gilbertson, *Social Workers as Expert Witnesses*, Nat'l Assoc. Social Workers 4-6 (2004) [hereinafter *Expert Witnesses*] (this law note may be purchased from NASW).

206 759 A.2d 755 (Md. 2000).

207 *See* Brief of Amici Curiae National Association of Social Workers, et al., *In re Adoption, Guardianship No. CCJ14746*, 759 A.2d 755 (Md. 2000) (No. 134).

208 For a more complete discussion see National Association of Social Workers Legal Defense Fund, *Are Licensed Clinical Social Workers Authorized to Provide Expert Witness Testimony Concerning the Diagnosis and Treatment of Emotional and Mental Disorders?* (2002), *at* https://www.socialworkers.org/ldf/legalissue/200202.asp (last visited Aug. 3, 2006) (this article is available online to NASW members).

209 *Id.*

210 A subpoena is a mandate, lawfully issued in the name of the court, compelling the attendance of an individual as a witness and/or the production of documents or things to the court. For a discussion of the legal and ethical obligations of social workers concerning subpoenas see Carolyn I. Polowy & Joel Gilbertson, *Social Workers and Subpoenas*, Nat'l Assoc. Social Workers (1997) [hereinafter *Subpoenas*] (this law note may he purchased from NASW).

211 Fed. R. Civ. P. 45(c)(3)(B)(ii).

212 *Subpoenas, supra* note 213, at 11.

213 Privileged communication is a statement made between persons in a protected relationship, such as attorney and client, priest and penitent, or psychotherapist and patient. For a discussion of a confidentiality and privileged communications between social workers and their clients see ; Carolyn I. Polowy & Carol Gorenburg, *Client Confidentiality and Privileged Communications*, Nat'l Assoc. Social Workers (1997) [hereinafter *Client Confidentiality*](this law note may be purchased from NASW).

214 518 U.S. 1 (1996).

215 *Expert Witnesses, supra* note 208, at 7.

216 Jaffee v. Redmond, 518 U.S. 1, 17 (1996).

217 National Association of Social Workers, *Code of Ethics* § 1.07 (revised 1999) ("Privacy and Confidentiality"), *available at* http://www.socialworkers.org/pubs/code/code.asp (last visited Aug. 3, 2006).

218 *See id.* at §1.07(b) (stating that "social workers may disclose confidential information where appropriate with valid consent from a client or a person legally authorized to consent on behalf of a client").

219 *See id.* at § 1.07(c). *See also* Tarasoff v. Regents of the University of California, 551 P.2d 334 (Cal. 1976) (recognizing the duty of a psychotherapist to protect a third party from the foreseeable harm of a client).

220 *See id.* at § 1.07(j). For example, all states require that a mental health professional report known or suspected cases of child abuse or neglect.

221 For further information on asserting and waiving privilege see *Subpoenas, supra* note 213; *Client Confidentiality, supra* note 216.

222 *Landis, supra* note 195, at §I (quoting Goodman v. Goodman, 141 N.W.2d 445 (Neb. 1966).

223 Uniform Marriage and Divorce Act §402, 9A U.L.A. 561 (1987); Krause, *supra* note 9, at 476-82. *See also* Shannon Dean Sexton, Note, *A Custody System Free of Gender Preferences and Consistent with the Best Interests of the Child. Suggestions for a More Protective and Equitable Custody System*, 88 Ky. LJ. 761, 770-71 (1999-2000); Andrea G. Nadel, Annotation, *Primary Caretaker Role of Respective Parents as Factor in Awarding Custody of Child*, 41 A.L.R.4th 1129, §2 (2005).

[224] *Guidelines for Child Custody Evaluations in Divorce Proceedings,* 49 No. 7 Am. Psycho'. 677-680 (1994), *available at* http://www.apa.org/practice/childcustody.html (last visited Aug. 3, 2006). *See also, Louisiana State Board of Social Work Examiners Guidelines for Child Custody Evaluations, at* http:www.labswe.org/child.htm (originally published July 1998).

[225] D. W. O'Neill, Annotation, *Child's Wishes as Factor in Awarding Custody,* 4 A.L.R3d 1396, §l[a] (2005).

[226] *See id., §2[a].*

[227] *Id.* at §13. *See, e.g.,* Rogers v. Rogers, 345 So.2d 1368 (Ala. Ct. App. 1977).

[228] *Id.* at §14.

[229] *Id.* at §15.

[230] 610 A.2d 999 (Pa. Super. Ct. 1992).

[231] *Id.* at 122-23. *See, e.g.,* Wooley v. Schoop, 12 N.W.2d 597 (Iowa 1944) (disregarding child's preference to live with stepfather rather than father where there was no evidence that father was unfit).

[232] Sheri A. Ahl, *A Step Backward: The Minnesota Supreme Court Adopts a "Primary Caretaker" Presumption in Child Custody Cases:* Pikula v. Pikula, 70 Minn. L. Rev. 1344, 1347 (1985-86).

[233] The varying treatments of the maternal preference rule include: (1) the mother, as a general rule, is preferred to the father in custody decisions; (2) neither parent is entitled to a preference; (3) the maternal preference rule governs absent a showing of unfitness of the mother; (4) the maternal preference may only be overcome by compelling evidence paternal custody would be in the child's best interest; and (5) the maternal preference is applicable where all other factors are equal. *See generally* Thomas R. Trenkner, Annotation, *Modern Status of Maternal Preference Rule or Presumption in Child Custody Cases,* 70 A.L.R.3d 262 (2005) (discussing the varying modern treatments of the maternal preference rule).

[234] *See* Ahl, *supra* note 232, at 1355.

[235] Some jurisdictions have created a legal presumption, either expressly or by implication, in favor of awarding custody to the primary caretaker of a child of "tender years." Nadel, *supra* note 226, at §3. The rationale behind the presumption is that it furthers the child's best interests by "guarantee[ing] stability, a sense of security, adaptation, and happiness." *Id.* However, critics of the primary caretaker presumption argue that the primary caretaker's ability to produce a stable environment prior to divorce does not necessarily correlate to stability following divorce. *Id.*

[236] Relevant factors for the court concerning a joint custody decree may include (1) agreement of the parties; (2) the parties ability to cooperate in making decisions concerning the child; (3) geographic proximity of the parental homes; (4) similarity between the parental home environments; (5) work hours of the parents; and (6) the wishes of the child. *See* Vitauts M. Gulbis, *Propriety of Awarding Joint Custody of Children,* 17 A.L.R.4th 1013, §3 (2005).

[237] *See* Colo. Rev. Stat. §14-10-124; Mont. Code Ann. §40-4-212; N.Y. Dom. Rel. Law §240; N.D. Cent. Code §1409-06.2; R.I. Gen. Laws §15-5-16; S.C. Code Ann. §20-3-160;

[238] Joint *legal* custody is generally defined as both parents having equal rights and responsibilities for major decisions concerning the child, including decisions about education, health care, and religious training. Jo-Ellen Paradise, Note, *The Disparity between Men and Women in Custody Disputes: Is Joint Custody the Answer to Everyone's Problems?,* 72 St. John's L. Rev. 517, 539-40 (1998). *See, e.g.,* Ala. Code §30-3-151(2). Joint *physical* custody is generally defined as the situation where the physical residence of the child is shared by the parents. Joint physical custody is often encouraged in order to promote frequent and continuing contact between the child and both parents. *See Joint Custody and Shared Parenting Statutes* (stating that "most states have adopted laws to encourage the involvement of both parents" through "frequent and continuing contact" with both parents), *at* http://www.gocrc.com/research/legislation.html (last updated Jan. 29, 2005). However, critics argue that it is not in a child's best interests due to a "lack of parental cooperation, continuing conflict between the parents, children experiencing instability when shuttled between homes, and logistical difficulties for parents." Lila Shapero, *The Case Against a Joint Custody Presumption,* 27-DEC Vt. B. J. 37, 37 (2001).

[239] *See* Alaska Stat. §25.20.060(c); Ark. Code Ann. §9-13-101(b)(1)(A)(ii); Del. Code Ann. tit. 13 §728; Fla. Stat. Ann. §61.046(15); 750 Ill. Comp. Stat. 5/602; Ind. Code Ann. §31-17-2-13; Ky. Rev. Stat. Ann. §403.270(5); La. Rev. Stat. Ann. §9:335; Me. Rev. Stat. Ann. tit. 19-A, §1653(2)(A) ("shared parental rights"); Md. Code Ann., Fam. Law §5-203; Mich. Comp. Laws

Ann. §722.26a; Neb. Rev. Stat. Ann. §42-364(5); Nev. Rev. Stat. Ann. §125.490(1); N.M. Stat, Ann. §40-4-9.1(J); N.C. Gen. Stat. §50-13.2; Ohio Rev. Code Ann. §3109.04(A)(2) ("shared parenting"); Or. Rev. Stat. §107.105; Tenn. Code Ann. §36-6-101; Tex. Fam. Code Ann. §101.016 ("joint managing conservatorship"); W. Va. Code Ann. §48-9-207; Wyo. Stat. Ann. §20-3-201(d).

[240] *See* Ala. Code §30-3-151; Ariz. Rev. Stat. Ann. §25-402(1); Cal. Fam. Code §3002; Conn. Gen. Stat. Ann. §46b-56a ; Ga. Code Ann. §19-9-6; Haw. Rev. Stat. Ann. §571-46.1(b); Idaho Code §32-717B(1); Mass. Gen. Laws Ann. ch. 208, §31; Minn. Stat. Ann. §518.003(Subd. 3); Miss. Code Ann. §93-5-24(5)(a); Mo. Ann. Stat. §452.375(1); Okl. Stat. Ann. tit. 43, §109(B); Utah Code Ann. §30-3-10.1; Vt. Stat. Ann. tit. 15, §664; Va. Code Ann. §20-124.1; Wis. Stat. Ann. §767.24(2).

[241] *See* Ind. Code Ann. §31-17-2-13 ("The court may award legal custody of a child jointly"); Iowa Code Ann. §598.1 ("'Joint custody' or 'joint legal custody' means an award of legal custody of a minor to both parents jointly under which both parents have legal custodial rights and responsibilities toward the child.") (The statute further defines "joint physical care" and gives the court discretion to provide for the *physical* care of the child); Kan. Stat. Ann. §16-601610(4) (allowing judicial discretion in awarding joint *legal* custody and the types of "residential arrangements," including "divided" residency); N.H. Rev. Stat. Ann. §458:17(III) ("[J]oint custody shall include all parental rights with the exception of physical custody which shall be awarded as the court deems most conducive to the benefit of the children.").

[242] *See* Cal. Fam. Code §3085 ([C]ourt may grant joint legal custody without granting joint physical custody."); Conn. Gen. Stat. Ann. §46b-56a (The court may award joint legal custody without awarding joint physical custody.-); D.C. Code Ann. §16-914 ("A custody order *may* include:...(iii) joint legal custody; (iv) joint physical custody...") (emphasis added); Haw. Rev. Stat. Ann. §571-46.1(b) (Custody order "may award joint legal custody without awarding joint physical custody."); Idaho Code §32-717B(1) ("The court may award either joint physical custody or joint legal custody or both..."); Me. Rev. Stat. Ann. tit. 19-A, §1653(2)(D)(1) (stating that court may award allocated, shared, or sole parental rights and responsibilities); Mich Stat. Ann. §722.26a ([T]he court *may... provide* that physical custody be shared by the parents"(emphasis added); Nev. Rev. Stat. Ann. §125.490(2) ("The court may award joint legal custody without awarding joint physical custody"); N.J. Stat. Ann. §9:2-4(a) ("[C]ourt shall enter an order which may include...[j]oint custody of a minor child...which is comprised of legal custody or physical custody"); 23 Pa. Cons. Stat. Ann. §5302 (A court may grant a shared custody order "awarding shared legal or physical custody, or both, of a child"); S.D. Codified Laws §25-5-7.1 (an award of joint custody includes the possibility of physical custody); Tex. Fam. Code Ann. §153.135 ("Joint managing conservatorship does not require the award of equal or nearly equal periods of physical possession of and access to the child"); Wash. Rev. Code Ann. §26.09.184 (a permanent parenting plan may allocate decision-making authority to one or both parents); Wyo. Stat. Ann. §20-2-201(d) ("Custody...may include any combination of joint, shared or sole custody.").

[243] *See* Cal. Fam. Code §3080; Conn. Gen. Stat. Ann. §46b-5a(b); Me. Rev. Stat. Ann. tit. 19-A, §1653(2)(A); Miss. Code Ann. §93-5-24(4); Nev. Rev. Stat. Ann. §125.490(1); N.H. Rev. Stat. Ann. §458:17(11)(a); Tenn. Code Ann. §36-6-101(a)(2)(A); Vt. Stat. Ann. tit. 15, §666.

[244] *See* Paradise, *supra* note 241, at 560 n. 233. *See infra* Appendix E. Critics argue that a joint custody presumption "ignores the need for continuity in a child's life by overlooking past child-rearing practices in which one parent exercised the bulk of child-rearing responsibility and imposing a structure giving both parents equal decision making power and/or equal physical care of the children." Shapero, *supra* note 241, at 37. Furthermore, mandating joint custody between parents may not end conflict between parents, and continuing conflict often leads to continuing court intervention. *Id.* Proponents of joint custody argue that it benefits the child by easing the pain of divorce through continuing contact with both parents, benefits the father by allowing him the opportunity to remain involved in the children's lives while enhancing the father-child bond, and benefits the mother because, by sharing parenting responsibilities, she can work outside the home, gain further education, and develop personal relationships. Stephanie N. Barnes, Comment, *Strengthening the Father-Child Relationship through a Joint Custody Presumption*, 35 Willamette L. Rev. 601, 602-03 (1999). *See also* Margaret F. Brinig & F.H. Buckley, *Joint Custody: Bonding and Monitoring Theories*, 73 Ind. L.J. 393, 402-407 (1998) (stating that joint custody may help lower the divorce rate because "fathers permit themselves to grow more attached to children when they do not fear a complete break with them on divorce[, and with the increased emotional ties, divorce becomes less likely").

245 See infra "Consent to Treatment and Disclosure of Confidential Information".

246 National Association of Social Workers, Code of Ethics §1.03(a), (c) (revised 1999) ("Informed Consent"), available at http://www.socialworkers.org/pubs/code/code.asp (last visited Aug. 3, 2006).

247 2005 WL 33388880 (Me. Super. Ct. 2005).

248 See infra, Appendix E, for a list of state statutes concerning non-custodial parent access to records.

249 See Ala. Code §30-3-154; Alaska Stat. §25.20.130; Ariz. Rev. Stat. Ann. §25-403(H); Cal. Fam. Code §3025; Colo. Rev. Stat. §14-10-123.8; D.C. Code Ann. §16-914(a)(I)(B)(i); Fla. Stat. Ann. §61.13(2)(b)(3); Idaho Code §32-717A; 750 Ill. Comp. Stat. Ann. 5/602.I(e); Iowa Code Ann. §598.41(e); Kan. Stat. Ann. §16-60-1610(4)(B); La. Rev. Stat. Ann. §9:351; Me. Rev. Stat. Ann. tit. 19-A, §1653(2)(D)(4); Mich. Stat. Ann. §722.30; Minn. Stat. Ann. §518.17(Suhd. 3); Miss. Code Ann. §93-5-24(5); Mo. Stat. Ann. §452.375(10); Mont. Code Ann. §40-4-225; Nev. Rev. Stat. Ann. §125.520(2); N.J. Stat. Ann. §9:2-4.2; Ohio Rev. Code Ann. §3109.051(H)(1); S.D. Codified Laws §25-57.3; Vt. Stat. Ann. tit. 15, §670.

250 Ala. Code §30-3-154 (emphasis added).

251 See Ark. Code Ann. §9-13-301 (scholastic records); Conn. Gen. Stat. Ann. §46b-56(e) (academic, medical, hospital, or other health records); D.C. Code Ann. §16-914(a)(3)(C)(8) (educational, medical, psychiatric, and dental treatment records); Md. Code Ann., Fam. Law §9-104 (medical, dental, and educational records); Mass. Gen. Laws Ann. ch. 208, §31 (academic, medical, hospital, or other health records); Neb. Rev. Stat. Ann. §42-364(4) (education and medical records); N.M. Stat. Ann. §40-4-9.1(H) (medical, dental, and school records); 23 Pa. Cons. Stat. Ann. §5309 (medical, dental, religious, or school records); S.C. Code Ann. §20-7-100 (educational and medical records); Tenn. Code Ann. §36-6-110(a)(4), (5) (medical and academic records); Tex. Fam. Code Ann. §153.073 (medical, dental, psychological, and educational records); Va. Code Ann. §20-124.6 (academic or health records) (as amended by 2005 Va. Acts ch. 181); Wash. Rev. Code Ann. §26.09.225 (education and health care records); W. Va. Code Ann. §48-9-601 (educational, medical, and juvenile court records); Wyo. Stat. Ann. §20-201(e) (school, medical, dental, and mental health records).

252 Neb. Rev. Stat. Ann. §42-364(4) (emphasis added).

253 Those states include: Georgia, Hawaii, Indiana, Kentucky, New Hampshire, New York, North Carolina, North Dakota, Oklahoma, Oregon, Rhode Island, Utah.

254 Many of the statutes state that a non-custodial parent has equal access to records pertaining to his or her child unless otherwise prohibited by court order or statute. See, e.g., Ariz. Rev. Stat. Ann. §25-403(H) (stating that both parents have access to records "[u]nless otherwise provided by court order or law").

255 See Attorney Ad Litem v. Parents of D.K., 780 So.2d 301 (Fla. Dist. Ct. App. 2001) (in a child custody dispute); Bond v. Bond, 887 S.W.2d 558 (Ky. Ct. App. 1994) (in a child custody dispute); Nagle v. Hooks, 460 A.2d 49 (Md. 1983) (in a child custody dispute); S.C. v. Guardian Ad Litem, 845 So.2d 953 (Fla. Dist. Ct. App. 2003) (in a dependency proceeding); In re Adoption of Diane, 508 N.E.2d 837 (Mass. 1987) (in an adoption proceeding); In re M.P.S., 342 S.W.2d 277 (Mo. Ct. App. 1961) (in a neglect proceeding).

256 886 A.2d 980 (N.H. 2005).

257 Id. at 987.

258 Id.

259 Id. at 986. Citing Jaffee v. Redmond, 518 U.S. 1 (1996), the Supreme Court of New Hampshire further stated, "[T]he mere possibility of disclosure may impede development of the confidential relationship necessary for successful treatment…[It is] difficult if not impossible for [a psychotherapist] to function without being able to assure…patients of confidentiality and, indeed, privileged communication." Id.

260 Id.

[261] For further discussion of the *Berg* decision and confidentiality options available under HIPAA see National Association of Social Workers Legal Defense Fund, *Children's Rights to Confidentiality* (2005), *at* https://www.naswdc.org/ldf/legal_issue/200502.asp (last visited Aug. 3, 2006) (this article is available online to NASW members).

[262] *See supra* notes 144-149 and accompanying text.

[263] Robin Cheryl Miller, Annotation, *Child Custody and Visitation Rights Arising from Same-Sex Relation-ship*, 80 A.L.R.5th 1, 1 (2005).

[264] *See id.* at §3[a]. *See also In re* Guardianship of Olivia J., 101 Cal. Rptr. 2d 364 (1st Cir. 2000) (psychological parent); *In re* E.L.M.C., 100 P.3d 546 (Colo. Ct. App. 2004) (psychological parent); *In re* A.B., 818 N.E.2d 126 (Ind. Ct. App. 2004) (equitable parent); C.E.W. v. D.E.W., 845 A.2d 1146 (Me. 2004) (de facto parent); Gestl v. Frederick, 754 A.2d 1087 (Md. Ct. Spec. App. 2000) ("person acting as parent"); LaChapelle v. Mitten, 607 N.W.2d 151 (Minn. Ct. App. 2000); Scott v. Scott, 147 S.W.3d (Mo. Ct. App. 2004); V.C. v. M.J.B., 748 A.2d 539 (N.J. 2000) (psychological parent); A.C. v. C.B., 829 P.2d 660 (N.M. Ct. App. 1992); T.B. v. L.R.M., 786 A.2d 913 (Pa. 2001) (partner stood in loco parentis to child and possessed standing to bring action for custody of child).

[265] Brief of Amici Curiae Support Center for Child Advocates et al., T.B. v. L.R.M., 786 A.2d 913 (Pa. 2(X)1) (No. 92 WAP 2000) (stating that because children form strong psychological bonds to persons acting as parents it is in the best interests of children to award partial custody to the biological mother's same-sex partner).

[266] This is the case even where the child's biological parent had named the same-sex partner as the guardian of her children in the case of her death. *See* McGuffin v. Overton, 542 N.W.2d 288 (Mich. Ct. App. 1995) (awarding custody to the biological father who had established no relationship with the children prior to the biological mother's death and the children had lived for eight years with the mother's partner).

[267] *Cf.* Guardianship of Astonn H., 635 N.Y.S.2d (N.Y. 1995) (awarding custody to biological mother's same-sex partner instead of mother of biological mother's estranged husband, who was not the child's biological father).

[268] *See, e.g.,* Utah Code Ann. §30-3-35.

[269] Christopher Vaeth, *Denial or Restriction of Visitation Rights to Parent Charge with Sexually Abusing Child*, 1 A.L.R.5th 776, §2 (2004).

[270] *Id.*

[271] *Id.* at §2[b].

[272] *See* Ala. Code §30-3-4; Alaska Stat. §25.20.065; Ariz. Rev. Stat. Ann. §25-409; Ark. Code Ann. §9-13-103; Cal. Fam. Code §3104; Colo. Rev. Stat. Ann. §14-10-123.3; Conn. Gen. Stat. Ann. §46h-59; Del. Code Ann. tit. 13, §728; Fla. Stat. Ann. §752.01; Ga. Code Ann. §19-7-3; Hawaii Rev. Stat. Ann. §571-46.3; Idaho Code §32-719; Ill. Comp. Stat. Ann. 5/607(b)-(e); Ind. Code Ann. §31-17-5-1; Iowa Code Ann. §598.35; Kan. Stat. Ann. §60.1616(b); Ky. Rev. Stat. Ann. §405.021; La. Rev. Stat. Ann. §9:344; Me. Rev. Stat. Ann. tit. 19-A, §1803; Md. Code Ann., Fam Law §9102; Mass. Gen. Laws Ann. ch. 119, §39D; Mich. Stat. Ann. §722.27(b); Minn. Stat. Ann. §257C.08(Subd. 1); Miss. Code Ann. §93-16-1; Mo. Ann. Stat. §452.402; Mont. Code Ann. §40-9-102; Neb. Rev. Stat. Ann. §43-1802; Nev. Rev. Stat. Ann. §125C.050; N.H. Rev. Stat. Ann. §458:17-d; N.J. Stat. Ann. §9:2-7.1; N.M. Stat. Ann. §40-9-2; N.Y. Dom. Rel. Law §240; N.C. Gen. Stat. §50-13.2; N.D. Cent. Code §14-09-05.1; Ohio Rev. Code Ann. §3109.051(B)(1); Okla. Stat. Ann. tit. 43, §111.IA; Or. Rev. Stat. §109.119; 23 Pa. Cons. Stat. Ann. §5301; R.I. Gen. Laws §15-5-24.1; S.C. Code Ann. §20-7-420(33); S.D. Codified Laws §25-4-52; Tenn. Code Ann. §36-6-306; Tex. Fam. Code Ann. §153.433 (amended by 2005 Tex. Sess. Law Serv. Ch. 484 (H.B. 261) (Vernon's); Utah Code Ann. §30-5-2 (amended by 2005 Utah Laws Ch. 129 (H.B. 222); Vt. Stat. Ann. tit. 15, §1011; Va. Code Ann. §20-124.2(B); Wash. Rev. Code Ann. §26.09.240: W. Va. Code Ann. §48-10-101; Wis. Stat. Ann. §767.245; Wyo. Stat. Ann. §207-101.

[273] *See generally Visitation Rights of Person Other than Natural Parents or Grandparents*, 1 A.L.R.4th 1270

(2005) (outlining court cases and state statutes that allow interested parties to petition for visitation).

274 Troxel v. Granville, 530 U.S. 57 (2000) (plurality opinion).

275 See R.S.C. v. J.B.C., 812 So.2d 361 (Ala. Civ. App. 2001); Seagrave v. Price, 79 S.W.3d 339 (Ark. 2002); In re Marriage of Harris, 112 Cal. Rptr.2d 127 (Cal. Ct. App. 2001); Roth v. Weston, 789 A.2d 431 (Conn. 2002); Beagle v. Beagle, 678 So.2d 1271 (Fla. 1996); Clark v. Wade, 544 S.E.2d 99 (Ga. 2001); Santi v. Santi, 633 N.W.2d 312 (Iowa 2001); Brice v. Brice, 754 A.2d 1132 (Md. Ct. Spec. App. 2000); Heltzel v. Heltzel, 638 N.W.2d 123 (Mich. Ct. App. 2001); Wilde v. Wilde, 775 A.2d 535 (N.J. Super. Ct. App. Div. 2001); Camburn v. Smith, 586 S.E.2d 565 (S.C. 2003); Currey v. Currey, 650 N.W.2d 273 (S.D. 2002); In re Parentage of C.A.M.A., 109 P.3d 405 (Wash. 2005); In re Paternity of Roger D.H., 641 N.W.2d 440 (Wis. Ct. App. 2002).

276 Krause, supra note 9, at 734 n. 7 (citing N.D. Cent. Code §14-09-05.1; Or. Rev. Stat. §109.119; Tenn. Code Ann. §30-5-2; Utah Code Ann. §30-5-2).

277 Krause, supra note 9, at 733-34 n. 6c (citing Roth v. Weston, 789 A.2d 431 (Conn. 2002); Clark v. Wade, 544 S.E.2d 99 (Ga. 2001); Kan. Dept. of Soc. & Rehab. Serv. v. Paillet, 16 P.3d 962 (Kan. 2001); Zeman v. Stanford, 789 So.2d 798 (Miss. 2001); Adams v. Tessener, 550 S.E.2d 499 (N.C. 2001); Neal v. Lee, 14 P.3d 547 (Okla. 2000); State ex rel Brandon L. v. Moats, 551 S.E.2d 674 (W. Va. 2001).

278 Krause, supra note 9, at 733 n. 6b (citing Rideout v. Riendeau, 761 A.2d 291 (Me. 2000); Hertz v. Hertz, 291 A.D. 91 (N.Y. 2002); In re Roger D.H., 641 N.W.2d 440 (Wis. Ct. App. 2002).

279 Thus, parents cannot contract to reduce or eliminate a child's right to support. Such a contract would be void against public policy. See, e.g., Straub v. B.M.T., 645 N.E.2d 597 (Ind. 1994).

280 In the United States, the age of majority traditionally was 21. However, in the past twenty years, most states have lowered the age of majority to 18.

281 See Cal. Fam. Code §3901; Del. Code Ann. tit. 13, §501(d).

282 See Tenn. Code Ann. §34-1-102; Tex. Fam. Code Ann. §154.001(a).

283 See N.Y. Dom. Rel. Law §240.

284 See, e.g., Neudecker v. Neudecker, 577 N.E.2d 960 (Ind. 1991).

285 See, e.g., Del. Code Ann. tit. 13, §501(b); Wash. Rev. Code Ann. §26.16.205.

286 See S.C. Code Ann. §20-7-936.

287 See generally Sara R. David, Turning Parental Rights into Parental Obligations—Holding Same-Sex Non-Biological Parents Responsible for Child Support, 39 New Eng. L. Rev. 921 (2005).

288 "In loco parentis" means that an individual has assumed all obligations incident to the parental relationship and is, therefore, liable for the same obligations as a biological parent. For example, in L.S.K. v. H.A.N., the court noted that it would he inequitable to award child visitation and custody to a non-biological parent without also obligating the party to 7day child support. L.S.K. v. H.A.N., 813 A.2d 872 (Pa. Super. Ct. 2002).

289 See, e.g., id.

290 A person is a "de facto parent" if that person assumed the day-to-day role of a parent in relation to the child. Judges will often look to duration of the parent-child relationship, the age and understanding of the child, and whether there would he a detriment to the child if was left solely with the biological parent.

291 For a discussion of the cases involving the various legal theories see Robin Miller, Child Support Obligations of Former Same-Sex Partners. 5 A.L.R.6th 303 (2005).

292 Id. at §9. See, e.g., Karin T. v. Michael T., 484 N.Y.S.2d 780 (N.Y. Fam. Ct. 1985).

293 2002 WL 1940145 (Del. Fam. Ct. 2002).

294 Id. at *10.

295 Id.

296 See Maria B. v. Superior Court, 97 P.3d 72 (Cal. 2004); T.F. v. B.L., 813 N.E.2d 1244 (Mass. 2004).

297 Erin J. May, Note, *Social Reform for Kentucky's Judicial System: The Creation of Unified Family Courts*, 92 Ky. L.J. 571, 574 (2003/2004) (calling for a unified family court process in Kentucky).

298 *Id.* at 275-77 (discussing how "a final resolution to [family related] problems may be substantially delayed due to the numerous judicial proceedings," and how a lack of coordination among cases may cause a child or family to make repetitive court appearances and lead to a fragmented judicial system).

299 See, e.g., D.C. Code Ann. §11-1101; Haw. Rev. Stat. Ann. §571-11, -14; N.Y. Fam. Ct. Act §115.

300 See, e.g., Haw. Rev. Stat. Ann. §571-12 (stating that all criminal cases where a minor was less than eighteen years old when the minor allegedly committed the offense shall be transferred to the Family Court).

301 Del. Code Ann. tit. 10, §921, 922. *See also* **http://courts.delaware.gov/Courts/Family%20 Court/** (last visited Aug. 3, 2006) (discussing the jurisdiction of the Delaware State Family Court).

302 See, e.g., D.C. Code Ann. §11-1102 (stating "to the greatest extent practicable and safe, cases and proceedings in the Family Court of the Superior Court shall be resolved through alternative dispute resolution procedures, in accordance with such rules as the Superior Court may promulgate").

303 *See The Family Court Vision, at* **http://www.in.gov/judiciary/family-court/about.html** (last modified Feb. 15, 2006) (discussing the Indiana Family Court Project's goals of "emphasizing a holistic and non-adversarial approach to problem solving").

304 *See infra* notes 43, 44 and accompanying text.

305 *See* 42 Am. Jur. 2d Infants §163.

306 *See infra* Appendix C for a list of pertinent state statutes concerning the appointment of a guardian *ad litem* in various types of proceedings.

307 *See* Fla. R. Civ. P. 1.210(b) ("The court shall appoint a guardian *ad litem* for an infant or incompetent person not otherwise represented in an action..."); Kan. Stat. Ann. §60-217(c) ("The court shall appoint a guardian *ad litem* for a minor or incapacitate person not otherwise represented in an action..."); Mich. Ct. R. 2.201(E) ("If the minor or incompetent person does not have a conservator to represent the person as defendant, the action may not proceed until the court appoints a guardian *ad litem*..."); Minn. R. Civ. P. 17.02 ("A party who is an infant or is incompetent and is not so represented shall be represented by a guardian *ad litem* appointed by the court in which the action is pending or is to be brought."); N.D. Cent. Code §14-10-04 ("A minor may enforce the minor's rights by civil action or other legal proceeding in the same manner as an adult, except that a guardian *ad litem* must be appointed to conduct the same."); Tenn. R. Juv. P. 37, §37-1-149 ("The court at any stage of a proceeding under this part, on application of a party or on its own motion, shall appoint a guardian *ad litem* for a child who is a party to the proceeding if such child has no parent, guardian or custodian appearing on such child's behalf..."); Wis. Stat. Ann. §803.01(3) ("A guardian *ad litem* shall be appointed in all cases where the minor or incompetent has no general guardian of property, or where the general guardian fails to appear and act on behalf of the ward or incompetent, or where the interest of the minor or incompetent is adverse to that of the general guardian.").

308 See, e.g., Mc. Rev. Stat. Ann. tit. 19-A, §1507 (stating that a "court *may* appoint a guardian *ad litem* when the court has reason for special concern as to the welfare of a minor child") (emphasis added). The Maine statute further provides the court with factors with which to determine whether an appointment should be made. Those factors include: the wishes of the parties, the age of the child, the nature of the proceeding, the financial resources of the parties, the extent to which a guardian *ad litem* may assist in providing information concerning the best interest of the child, whether the family has experiences a history of domestic abuse, and any other factors the court determines relevant. *Id.*

309 42 Am. Jur. 2d Infants §163.

310 *Id.*

311 See, e.g., 750 Ill. Comp. Stat. Ann. 5/506 ("The guardian *ad litem* shall testify or submit a written report to the court regarding his or her recommendations in accordance with the best interest of the child."); N.D. Cent. Code §40-4-8 ("If appointed, a guardian *ad litem* shall serve as an advocate of the children's best interests."); Wis. Stat. Ann. §767.045(4) ("The guardian *ad litem* shall be an advocate for the best inter-

ests of a minor child as to paternity, legal custody, hysical placement, and support.").

[312] See, e.g., Alaska Stat. §25.24.310 ("[T]he court may…appoint an attorney *or other person* or the office of public advocacy to provide guardian *ad litem* services to a child in any legal proceedings involving the child's welfare.").

[313] See Minn. R. Guardian *Ad Litem* P. 2, *available at* http://www.courts.state.mn.us/rules/adlitem. html (last visited Aug. 3, 2006) ("Before a person may be recommended for service as a guardian *ad litem* pursuant to Rule 4, the person must satisfy the following minimum qualifications…(h) have satisfactorily completed the pre-service training requirements…and demonstrated a comprehension of the responsibilities of guardians *ad litem*…). *See also* Standards to Govern the Appointment of Guardians *Ad Litem* (Children), *available at* http://www.courts.state.va.us/1/cover.htm (last modified Oct. 3, 2002) ("The Judicial Council of Virginia…sets forth the following standards to govern the appointment of lawyers as guardians *ad litem* pursuant to §16.1-266," which include the completion of "seven hours of MCLE approved continuing legal education…in order to initially comply with these standards and be included in on the list of qualified attorneys…").

[314] See, e.g., 750 Ill. Comp. Stat. Ann. 5/506 ("[T]he court may…appoint an *attorney* to serve in one of the following capacities to address the issues the court delineates:…(2) Guardian *ad litem*.").

[315] A discussion of concerns about the appointment of guardians *ad litem* on a county-by-county basis can be found in Office of the Legislative Auditor, State of Minnesota, Program Evaluation Division, *Guardians ad Litem* (Feb. 28, 1995), *available at* http://www.auditor.leg.state.mn.us/ped/1995/ GUARDSUM.HTM (last visited Aug. 3, 2006) (stating that "Minnesota is one of 33 states where guardian services are provided locally).

[316] See infra Appendix C for a list of pertinent state statutes concerning the appointment of a guardian *ad litem* in contested divorce-related proceedings.

[317] Ala. Code §26-2A-52; Alaska Stat. §25.24.310; Fla. Stat. Ann. §61.401; Haw. Rev. Stat. Ann. §571-46; 750 Ill. Comp. Stat. Ann. 5/506; Ind. Code Ann. §31-15-6-1; Iowa Code Ann. §598.12; Me. Rev. Stat. Ann. tit. 19-A, §1507; Mass. Gen. Laws Ann. ch. 215, §56A; Mich. Comp. Laws Ann. §722.27(1)(d); Minn. Stat. Ann. §518.165; Mo. Ann. Stat. §452.423; Mont. Code Ann. §40-4-205; N.J. Stat. Ann. §9:2-4(c); N.M. Stat. Ann. §40-4-8; N.D. Cent. Code §14-09-06.4; Ohio R. Civ. P. 75(B)(2); R.I. Gen. Laws §15-5-16.2(c); Tex. Fam. Code Ann. §107.001; Va. Code Ann. §16.1-266; Wis. Stat. Ann. §767.045.

[318] Fla. Stat. Ann. §61.401 ("In such action which involve an allegation of child abuse, abandonment, or neglect…the court shall appoint a guardian *ad litem* for the child."); Minn. Stat. Ann. §518.165(Subd. 2) ("[I]f the court has reason to believe that the minor child is a victim of domestic child abuse or neglect…the court shall appoint a guardian *ad litem*."); Mo. Ann. Stat. §452.423 ("The court shall appoint a guardian *ad litem* in any proceeding in which child abuse or neglect is alleged."); Va. Code Ann. §16.1-266 ("Prior to the hearing by the court of any case involving a child who is alleged to be abused or neglected…the court shall appoint a discreet and competent attorney-at-law as guardian *ad litent*…").

[319] Alaska Stat. §25.24.310; Ariz. Rev. Stat. Ann. §25-321; Cal. Fam. Code §3150; Colo. Rev. Stat. Ann. §14-10-116; Conn. Gen. Stat. Ann. §46b-54; Del. Code Ann. tit. 13, §721(c); D.C. Code Ann. §16-918(); Fla. Stat. Ann. §61.401; 750 Ill. Comp. Stat. Ann. 5/506; Ind. Code Ann. §31-15-6-1; Iowa Code Ann. §598.12; Ky. Rev. Stat. Ann. §403.090; La. Rev. Stat. Ann. §9:345; Md. Code Ann., Fam. Law §1-202; Neb. Rev. Stat. Ann. §42-358(1); Ohio R. Civ. P. 75(B)(2); Okla. Stat. Ann. tit. 10, §24; Pa. R. Civ. P. 1915.11; R.I. Gen. Laws §15-5-16.2(c); S.D. Codified Laws §25-4-45.4; Tex. Fam. Code Ann. §107.001; Utah Code Ann. §30-3-11.2; Vt. Stat. Ann. tit. 15, §594; Va. Code Ann. §16.1-266.

[320] La. Rev. Stat. Ann. §9:345 ("The court shall appoint an attorney to represent the child if…any party presents a prima facie case that a parent or other person caring for the child has sexually, physically, or emotionally abused the child…").

[321] Alaska Stat. §25.24.310 ("Instead of, or in addition to, appointment of an attorney…the court may…appoint an attorney or other person or the office of public advocacy to provide guardian *ad litem* services to a child in any legal proceeding involving the child's welfare."); Ariz. Rev. Stat. Ann. §8-535; Ariz. Rev. Stat. Ann. §25-321; Fla. Stat. Ann. §61.401 r[T]he court may appoint a guardian *ad litem* to act as next friend of the child…The court in its discretion may *also* appoint legal counsel for a child to act as attorney or advocate…"); 750 Ill. Comp. Stat. Ann. 5/506 ("The court

may…appoint an attorney to serve in one of the following capacities…(1) Attorney…(2) Guardian *ad litem*."); Ind. Code Ann. §31-15-6-1 ("A court… may appoint: (1) a guardian *ad litem;* (2) a court appointed special advocate; or (3) both; for a child at any time."); Iowa Code Ann. §598.12 (-The court may appoint an attorney to represent the legal interests of the minor child…The court may appoint a guardian *ad litem* to represent the best interests of the minor child…"); Ohio R. Civ. P. 75(B)(2) ("The court may…appoint a guardian *ad litem* and legal counsel, if necessary, for the child…"); R.I. Gen. Laws §15-5-16.2(c) ("The court may…appoint an attorney or a guardian *ad litem* to represent the interest of a minor…"); Tex. Fam. Code Ann. §107.001(2), (5); Va. Code Ann. §16.1-266 ("In all cases which…require counsel or a guardian *ad litem*, or both, to represent the child…attorneys-at-law may he appointed by the court.").

[322] *See, e.g.,* Me. Rev. Stat. Ann. tit. 19-A, §1507 (stating that "[title court may appoint a guardian *ad litem* when the court has reason for special concern as to the welfare of a minor child").

[323] *See, e.g., In re* Brown, 2002 WL 1454025 (Ohio Ct. App. July 3, 2002) (social worker testified concerning the termination of the parental rights of two minor children); *In re* Taylor, 1999 WL 417995 (Ohio Ct. App. June 11, 1999) (social worker testified concerning the permanent custody of two minor children); Sjodin v. Sjodin, 1997 WL 613663 (Minn. Cl App. Oct. 7, 1997) (social worker testified concerning the custody and visitation of the minor child).

[324] 658 S.2d 1378 (Miss. 1995).

[325] *Id.* at 1384.

[326] *See, e.g., id.* at 1383-84 (stating that whether to adhere to the recommendations of either the guardian *ad litem* or the social worker is determined by the "sound discretion of the chancellor").

[327] 831 So.2d 1179 (Miss. Ct. App. 2002).

[328] *Id.* at 1182.

[329] The social worker who files a dependency petition "shall be discussion in S.D. v. Anthony D., 125 Cal. Rptr. 570, so that only an independent guardian ad litem could he agency who filed the dependency petition, was an

[330] See Cal. R. Ct. 1438. The inter former Rule 1438 provided that the guardian *ad litem* to represent the interests of the "minor." *See* 572–573 (Cal. Ct. App. 2002). However, the statute was changed appointed, i.e., that the social worker, as the representative of the interested party in the case wan not independent. *Id.*

[331] 2004 WL 2931014 (Ohio Ct. App. Dec. 16, 2004).

[332] *Id.* At *2.

[333] *Id.*

[334] *Id.*

[335] *Id.* at 3.

[336] *See, e.g.* Ohio Rev. Code Ann. §2317.02.